Coming of Age
In California

Coming of Age
In California

Personal Essays

GERALD HASLAM

Foreword by **Floyd Salas**

DEVIL MOUNTAIN BOOKS
P.O. Box 4115
WALNUT CREEK, CALIFORNIA 94596

Various of these essays have appeared in *This World, The Californians, Health Care Update, California English, Network,* and *Amelia.* This collection was completed with the assistance of an Artist's Fellowship in Literature from the California Arts Council for which the author is most grateful.

GERALD HASLAM

Coming of Age in California

Personal Essays

DEVIL MOUNTAIN BOOKS, P.O. BOX 4115, WALNUT CREEK, CA 94596. ALL RIGHTS RESERVED.

Design and Cover / Wayne Gallup
Typestyle: Palatino

Library of Congress Cataloging-in-Publication Data

Haslam, Gerald W.
  Coming of age in California : personal essays / Gerald Haslam : foreword by Floyd Salas.
    p. cm.
  ISBN 0-915685-07-8 : $8.95
  1. Haslam, Gerald W.—Biography. 2. Authors, American—20th century—Biography. 3. California—Social life and customs.
  I. Title.
    PS3558.A724Z463   1990
    813'.54—dc20   89-81320
  [B]   CIP

23•5432

*For my mother and my father
and for James Baldwin*

CONTENTS

FOREWORD

Personal is the word for these essays. I felt deep emotion and was moved to tears by almost every piece in this collection. They don't teach or hammer a point, but reveal in the most honest way the background of this modest, gifted and good man. This is not a literary biography, but a revelation of self in public confession, without guilt, of humble beginnings that produced a literary man.

I'm reminded of James Baldwin, a superb writer of personal essays such as those in *Nobody Knows My Name* and *The Fire Next Time*, books that made me care for him and the black man in America. But Baldwin never made me feel as deeply, never provoked me to tears like these essays do. Baldwin was always concerned with making his didactic point about an abstraction while Haslam is concerned with the revelation of his very personal heart and he succeeds, whether talking of his Anglo-Latin ancestors, his schools and teachers, or himself.

Haslam writes about those he loved and still loves, dead or alive, with a clear and honest eye, and hides nothing about the humble individual human beings he sings of. It is his naked honesty that strikes so deep, that makes me care so much, honesty that makes the writing tough and never close to sentimental. He not only doesn't hide but celebrates the faults and virtues of these human beings within their working-class surroundings. These are not poor but successful people and admirable in their own right. Haslam gives you spiritual beings carried forward on the wave of his own spirit. He sees them with affection and what he writes about is their love and his love, which makes us love, too.

In "Pop" he describes how he takes care of his father, whose brain tissue is slowly dying, and reaches the heart of this undemonstrative man, who is so typical of that generation of American males who earned the meat and bread and left the raising of their kids to their wives. At the end he says, "I kneel in this the autumn of my life...and pat his weary back and say, 'It's all right, Pop. It's okay.' And it is."

In "An Affair of Love" Haslam tells with refreshing honesty

of the mixed Latino-Anglo background of his mother and his battle to give her love in spite of her madness in old age: "My strategy is simple, the very one she had used on me when I was small and vulnerable: more hugs, more kisses, more tender tones to fight her demons—no matter how coldly such entreaties are received—because love is all that matters between us. But not merely between us, and this is the lesson she has taught me: in the final analysis, love is the affair of life, the central issue of our existence."

Haslam can be fiercely tough, too, as in "Coming of Age in California," in which he tells of three generations of an ethnically mixed California family. His blond and fair daughter fights the good fight of love and tolerance when she encounters racism at a college party and shouts, "Hey...I'm a spic!" Words which will stand out in your mind. Tolerance is the topic, love of your fellow man is the real issue.

Like most Americans of pioneer stock, my grandfathers worked the land. One, a rancher, lost his money during the Great Depression and then picked crops, with his sons as his crew, on the land of other men. So I identified with "Reflections from an Irrigation Ditch" where Haslam tells how he had his feet in the mud, literally, as a child. But it's not exploitation but the love a child had for the California soil he worked which lingers in a beautifully realized piece of nostalgia.

This love extended to his school and his student friends in "Brothers' Boy," a pleasant memory of Catholic training, and "Portrait of a Pal," about an athletic friend, call him Spitfire Meyer, who became a Christian Brother and later a winegrower, but as a middle-aged man could still take care of a loud-mouthed punk. "For reasons neither Meyer nor I understood or cared about then, most of our other pals were Mexican-Americans—rowdy, randy guys devoid of snootiness." The theme remains love.

Haslam also explores ritualistic—possibly sacramental—elements of football in "Bloodrites" and explains something of his larger motivation in "Writing About Home." In this, the last essay, he suggests, "Home is the place you cannot leave no matter where you go." Clearly, he has not left.

In "Homage to Uncle Willie," Haslam tells of his love for a

male ancestor. It's touching from the first page, which is deep and powerful, and amazingly gutty in the recounting of his wiping his dying uncle's butt. But it is also humorous when he describes in his uncle's girlfriend's dialog how she peed in a bucket during a row on a lake. And in "Growing Up at Babe's," Haslam fondly remembers his friend and weight coach, Babe Cantieny.

"Denouement" begins with a moving first paragraph about his wife: "This beautiful woman is my closest friend, the one indispensable ingredient in my life, and she loves me. How in the world did it happen?" I cried when, with his wife and son at his side, they buried their dog. And when his wife demands a kiss from him in the early morning, Haslam made my own life seem much more worth living. Few writers have such skill.

Floyd Salas

Coming of Age In California

Personal Essays

POP

I shrug my father off my back, unclasp his arthritic fingers from my heart, and let him drop like a knapsack. Momentarily, I am lighter, my feet floating from the ground with each stride, then I turn and see him as he had once seen me — toothless, incontinent, frightened.

He gazes toward me, lost, brows furrowing, then at last he grins: "Hi, Gerry."

Pop has been stripped of the ability to protect his feelings, so his smile reaches deep into me — he is genuinely happy to recognize his son. When he is troubled, that toothless mouth works toward a mask of tragedy and those eyes, almost depthless, dampen. He has become a man who *is* his emotions.

As a result of strokes, he suffers from physical debilitation and dementia. Cancer and arthritis also wrack him, and he wanders defenseless, though not totally oblivious, through a world that is no longer familiar. His position is summed up by a repeated complaint: "I can't even write a check." He can, of course, when he is with me — I fill it out for him, he laboriously signs — but he can not whiz to the Tejon Club, Oildale's primary blue-collar beer bar, and effortlessly cash one. He is no longer independent.

Last summer I took my father to a reunion in Santa Maria where he attended high school. A large, robust-looking man about his age approached us and extended his right hand. My father did the same, automatically but without recognition. When the man tried to speak with him, Pop could not respond, his eyes as dull as the case heads of shells in a shotgun's breech. For a moment the man gazed into my father's face, then he turned toward me, tears welling from his own eyes, and challenged, "I hope you *know* who this guy was. I hope you know he was student-body president. He was an All-American, for

Christ's sake. He stayed after practice to help the rest of us. I hope you know..." The man could not continue. I said nothing because, in truth, I *didn't* know and never can, what he represented to his peers.

When the big man spoke again, he seemed to have aged and he no longer sounded like he was confronting me. "Old Speck was the best," he said, then he shook my hand and wandered away. My father appeared not to have noticed him. He was extending his hand toward a much younger man who was passing by and who looked startled as he accepted it. In fact, Pop's right hand was extended all afternoon, as old chums or girlfriends lined up to greet him then slumped sadly away, or as kind-but-unnerved strangers accepted it. And he smiled, not recognizing them, but relishing the contact.

Among my oldest and fondest remembrances are of wrestling with my dad when I was a boy. I can't say exactly how old I was because our bouts continued from the time I was a toddler until I began high school, and they all merge in my mind into one frolic. It is my only clear recollection of physical contact with him during those years, and I protect it as I would a sliver from the true cross.

He is always young when we wrestle, always wearing a white T-shirt splattered with oil, always smelling vaguely of beer. He teaches me a hammerlock, a half nelson, an escape, for he was in his youth a competitive wrestler. He manipulates me over the rug or the grass, giving me the illusion of competition while alert not to hurt me, both of us laughing. My mother's face is troubled as she watches us. "Take it easy, Speck," she urges, "you'll get him all worked up."

That, unfortunately, is one of my few recollections of him during my earliest years. He resided at home but did not seem to live there. The arguments I used to hear rumbling through the walls in the night told me more about my folks' marriage than happy facades could hide. So did Mom's fragile emotions; she seemed as vulnerable as he did impervious. And theirs was in my memory never a relationship much livened by public displays of affection.

Pop was the black-sheep son of a black-sheep son; he was born in Texas where his father had been exiled for marrying a divorcee, Grandma. After her death in the great flu epidemic of 1919, Grandpa had remarried a woman remembered without warmth by everyone in the family and, as my father's sister Betty explains, a confrontation was inevitable. "When he was thirteen, Speck walked into a bedroom where our stepmother was whacking the daylights out of Bill and me with a buggy whip. Speck jerked the whip out of her hand and gave her a good beating. Then he left and never lived at home again."

"He never forgot or forgave his stepmother," adds his half sister, Isabel. "She had an enemy for life, maybe because Speck somehow blamed her for Momma's death or for taking Momma's place, I don't know. I think he had trouble really liking women after that. And I don't think he much respected the father who remarried either." She shakes her head sadly.

"Momma's death scarred him," theorizes his younger brother, Bill. "He was just a little kid, but he must've determined at some level never to allow himself to be that vulnerable again. Or maybe he just figured nothing could ever hurt him worse than that, so what the hell. It just seemed to hit him harder than it did the rest of us. He isn't the kind who can forget.

"Anyway, he just got tougher and tougher. He wasn't afraid of anyone or anything. He was pound-for-pound the strongest guy I ever knew, and was he fast — at UCLA he was the fastest on the team, and he's got the trophies to prove it. He'd compete at anything — swamping sacks of potatoes onto a truckbed or shooting pool. Put that together with the way he wouldn't spare himself, and you've got someone to contend with."

Uncle Bill sighs, remembering the brother who once awed him. He is himself an open, loving man who does not harbor grudges. "Poor Speck has never been able to forgive things easily. He still hates our stepmother with a passion. He can't get her out of his craw." She died last fall, nearly 100 years old.

Once in awhile, Pop would take me to work with him at the Shell Oil tank farm north of Oildale, near Bakersfield, always introducing me to his pals as "my tax exemption," an appellation I did not figure out until I was well into my teens.

I liked it, in any case, because it was something special between us. After work, he would stop at the Tejon Club to drink beer with other working men, laugh, perhaps shoot snooker. He'd buy me a soft drink and allow me to sip the foam from his draft. And he always seemed happy there.

But there is an irony in his contentment with that company because my father had once been one of the golden boys of autumn, a UCLA football player who had touched a richer, more glamorous life — rubbed elbows with Joe E. Brown and Mike Frankovich, played bit parts in football movies — then unaccountably lost confidence and let it all slip away. He felt intense, festering dissatisfaction at not having graduated, at being stranded in a blue collar. This occasionally and ironically emerged in the form of sullen complaints about "big shots" and "phonies."

I did not understand college, myself, and identified it only with football. Throughout my childhood, Mom showed me old yearbooks, programs from UCLA football games, and clippings from Los Angeles newspapers — all of which were generally kept hidden in a cedar chest in my parents' bedroom. I was made aware that Pop had been an exceptional player, and I came to understand why he seemed happiest of all on those occasions when old teammates visited, drank, and reminisced.

He rarely talked about his college experience otherwise, not to me, at least. It was, I now suspect, like many other things in his life, so painful a memory that it had to be buried. Certainly, it was an enduring burden in his life, thus in ours, for he felt trapped in his job as a gauger in the Kern River oil fields, and it led him to stress education, however passively — no homework help from him, but a poor grade gained immediate negative attention. Like many other blue-collar people, he wanted me to eventually earn a degree but not to be much changed in the process. But that soft problem was years ahead and unimagined when I used to lie on the floor and revel in photographs of Pop slashing into opponents on the grass of the Los Angeles Coliseum.

I first saw my dad in action when I was about twelve and had already recognized that I was not a particularly formidable street fighter — a serious deficiency in Oildale then.

Two men in a car swerved off the street and onto our small front yard, where my mother was watering. The driver emerged from the vehicle and made a smart remark to her. I don't remember if she called Pop or not, but he was immediately outside, chest-to-chest with the malefactor. A moment later the larger man swung his right fist, only to promptly find himself on the ground with my father on top of him. The second man jumped on Pop who, in rapid, furious fashion, entangled him, and thrust him rudely to the soil, then said ominously something like, "Stay there until the police arrive or I'm going to have to hurt you." Both of them stayed. I heard Mr. Clark, a neighbor, later say to another neighbor, Mr. Tatum, "Those guys must not've known who Speck was."

Not all his lessons were so harsh. Once we stopped for supplies at a grocery store in Edison, a small, packing-shed town along Highway 58 east of Bakersfield. Several tired-looking men with bedrolls were squatting near the door. One of them, his eyes averted, said something to my dad, who emerged a few minutes later from the store with two bags of food, one of which he gave to them. Back in the car, he explained that those were working men out of work.

Another time, we were at Hart Park outside Bakersfield and Pop recognized a black man, "Mr. Allen," who stood with three children watching other folks enjoy the merry-go-round and small roller coaster. Mr. Allen was a seasonal laborer who occasionally toiled at the same farm where one of my uncles worked, and Pop guessed correctly that he had no money to purchase admission to the rides for his youngsters. Saying nothing, making no issue of it, my dad bought tickets for my cousin and myself and for those three children he had never seen before. In fact, all five of us rode everything that afternoon while Pop and the black man stood together. Despite occasional verbal relapses, Pop always seemed more concerned with people's quality than their color. "Is he a good guy?" was his major criterion.

Unfortunately, he was not always a positive model. He drank far too much and did not consistently control his ominous temper. I never saw him act violently at home, but I certainly heard him say brutal things. Moreover, when I married, the only advice he gave was, "Never tell your wife too much" — hardly a truth on which to build a relationship, but marriage was not his strong point, as he openly acknowledged.

He did not much acknowledge his athletic prowess and seemed determined not to encumber me with it. Nonetheless, I knew that I could not, not ever, match it and I was ashamed. You see, my father, at only 165 pounds, had in the early 1930s been awarded honorable mention as a guard on the Walter Camp All-America Football Team. Typical of him, his certificate was not displayed but rested in that cedar chest in my folks' bedroom, but I knew it was there because my mother showed it to me. It also rested on my mind when I, too, played football — in junior high school, in high school, in college, and in the service. I pushed it ahead of me like Sisyphus's stone.

Not that my father pressured me about athletics; he didn't. But I felt I had to live up to his reputation, so when he actually came to watch me play football when I was a tenth grader, and I performed well, it was a major triumph. I heard him tell my mother, "No kiddin', he's really good." He said nothing to me. Unfortunately, he also saw my worst moment as a jock, a humiliating defeat in the finals of a boxing tournament and that time, liquor loosening his lips, he did say something that wounded me: "You didn't even try." In fact, I had tried as best my limited abilities would allow, but pugilism is an unforgiving sport.

When I was thirty or thirty-one, already the father of four children myself, we celebrated Christmas in our traditional fashion — three generations gathered at my aunt and uncle's house in Bakersfield. I acted as Santa Claus, handing out gifts. There was much laughter as Tom and Jerries were consumed and tongue-in-cheek presents were accepted with mock gravity. Late in the festivities, I handed Pop a package and my aunt laughingly called, "Give him a kiss, Speck, just like you did the grandchildren."

To my astonishment, he reached up and cupped my head in one powerful hand, pulled me forward and kissed my cheek. "I should've done that when you were little," he choked as our eyes met. It is the only time I can ever remember him kissing me, yet the emotion in his eyes told me how much he had always yearned to do it, and I at last understood the terrible trap within which he had lived. "Thanks Pop," was all I could manage to say.

In the general high spirits and hilarity of the gathering, few in the family noticed what had occurred, and today my father is no longer capable of remembering it, but to me it remains the single most important event of my life as his son.

This, then, is the man I have dropped from my back, this black-sheep son of a black-sheep son. And what am I? I am the boy who needed more than his father could give, and who felt in turn, that he could never give as much as his father deserved. I am the boy who once had to tell his dad that he could no longer drive an automobile, who has since had to chastise him for opening the door of a moving car, and who has now changed his father's diaper and washed his bottom. And I am the boy who has shrugged him from his back.

But I have not dropped this shriveled man in order to cast him away. No, indeed. Instead I kneel in this the autumn of my life and I embrace him, lift him to my heart as I have lifted my own sons and daughters, as he has lifted his grandchildren, and I pat his weary back gently and say, "It's all right, Pop. It's okay."

And it is.

AN AFFAIR OF LOVE

Mom insists, "Margie. *Margie!*"

Finally Aunt Marge aborts her conversation with me and turns toward my mother. "What *is* it, Sis?"

"Some days I don't get to talk to anybody at all." Mom's face is beyond hang-dog; it is hang-hound.

My own mask hardens because this is a message about me and for me: "My son leaves me alone. Some days no one visits me." I resist the impulse to respond.

"Whose fault is that?" snaps my aunt.

Mother does not reply. This is not what she had anticipated.

Aunt Marge continues. "You've got friendly neighbors on all sides of you. How many have you visited?"

Mother feathers her face with one hand and sighs, "My eyes..." She has lost some peripheral vision due to a stroke.

"Your eyes my eye!" Marge snaps. "You've got grandchildren over every single day. You're so lucky. Have you *ever* counted your blessings? If you'd stop sitting around feeling sorry for yourself, you'd have a social life. Have you *ever* visited one of your neighbors?"

Mom turns away. She does not answer. She is sitting with the two people in the world closest to her, her lone surviving sibling and her only child, but she is solitary. I touch her arm and she jerks, turns sick, shallow eyes toward me. "Huh?" she grunts.

Memories, Memories:

Mommy is reading Horton Hatches the Egg *while I curl on her lap. She points toward letters and asks their sounds. It is a game and I love it. In a family*

8

where books have been considered affectations and educa-
tion a luxury, she is gently trying to teach me to read
although I am not yet three.

Her sister is there, young and pretty, and she teases,
"Sis, you're spoiling him rotten."

Mom ignores her. "Can you spell your name for
Aunt Marge?"

"Gee-ee-ar-ar-wy," I declare, absolutely secure in her
love.

Mom laughs, scratches my head and kisses me, while
my aunt shakes her head and smiles. "He's so es-mart,"
she says in the Spanish-accent parody that characterizes
our family's intimate language.

My mother no longer initiates affection, no longer can, I
suspect. When I kiss her, she smacks me with one corner of
her lips like a person lying, this woman who lavished me with
love, who made me certain of my place in the world even when,
as it turns out, she was uncertain of her own. In large measure due to the assurance she instilled in me, I have been able
to break the family paradigm, to enter a wider world, pursue
education and career.

The sad irony is that precisely the self-esteem she instilled
has opened a chasm between us; she was not prepared for its
results. Never openly critical, she explains with quiet reproach,
"In *our* family *we* stayed home and took care of our folks. *We*
didn't move away." She does not mention that some of them,
unable to hold steady jobs, were in fact *supported* by aging parents.

Now my mother is an aging parent herself, one whose
son has pursued a life 300 miles from his hometown. Living
near us now, she believes, or says she believes, that she is a
displaced person, virtually kidnaped from the security of old
friends and familiar settings. Her wounds are open, her own
imperfect childhood haunting her as life constricts and pinches
closed. She is baffled, she is afraid, and often, she feels abandoned.

When she was four, her own mother suffering from severe asthma, Mom was shipped to San Francisco to live with

her maternal grandmother, Esperanza Terrill-Botella, and her step-grandfather, Jose Castillo. For the next ten years she lived in a home that also sheltered, off and on at least, three uncles and two cousins, plus the various wives and paramours of the uncles — a considerable parade, according to Mother.

The consequences of that long sojourn may not all be dark. When a couple of years ago Jonina Weeks, herself Hispanic, was writing a master's thesis on my fiction, she said, "All that hidden religion, that passion...the key to understanding your work is that you're more Spanish than even you know." Perhaps. Mixed ethnicity aside, my formative years were certainly dominated by a mother who spent her early years with a grandmother whose own mother migrated from Spain to Mexico, then to California. There are tendrils of magic still there, but how deep and how many is the question.

It was a classic example of *la familia*, a Hispanic Californian family: Spanish speaking but ethnically mixed, Roman Catholic in name if not practice, highly moral in public matters, less so in private, and given to easy outrage over the excesses of *los otros*, the others, outsiders, especially those same wives and paramours. (There was and remains a strong sense that her loved ones, including me, have been victimized by *los otros*.) It was, in any case, a busy, economically marginal household, with no one in a secure job, but everyone working some of the time. "I guess we were poor," she acknowledges, "but I didn't *feel* poor."

Today my mother is afraid of the dark, afraid of strangers, afraid of change. I asked her psychiatrist if that separation from family nearly seventy-five years ago might be haunting her. "What if you were four and put on a train and sent to a household that was strange, far away from your mother and father?" he asks. "She could have been abused there for all we know — she's got something buried in herself that won't go away."

Mom remembers those years with mixed emotions. Her grandmother was small, fair, square-faced, bald-headed and tart-tongued, and she kept money in tobacco bags pinned to her underskirts; she wore a black wig — her "transformation" my mother calls it. Aunt Marge adds another insight: Grandma

Esperanza, as she was called, never used gifts she received, but instead created a kind of shrine of them, new towels, bottles of cheap cologne, and bright beads enshrined in a corner of her upper Geary Street flat. Everyone agrees that she verbally dominated Grandpa Joe.

He was a dark mestizo with a sweeping handlebar mustache who, when he worked, tended bar in saloons. Grandma had divorced her first husband — "a red-haired Portugee named Silva," says Mom, who never saw him — and sent her own four children away to an orphanage while she struggled to survive as a sweatshop seamstress. How and where she and Grandpa Joe got together is another family mystery, but that henpecked man may have regretted it, since he constantly declared, *"Voy a volver a Chihuahua!"* — he was going to return to his native state — and my mother remembers crying and begging him not to leave. He never did.

They were actually affectionate sparring partners from all I can gather. Mom likes to tell about a time my great-grandmother, who was as usual rattling on in spitfire Spanish, had turned her back on Grandpa Joe, and he'd placed his thumb on the tip of his nose and slowly waved his fingers at her. She turned just in time to see him and snapped in clear English, "Oh, kiss your own ass you old fool!"

Jose Castillo died when I was a little boy and Grandma was devastated. She came and lived with us, but her considerable spirit was by then leaking and she was never the same. Only years later did my mother tell me that Grandma and Grandpa had never been married, a deep, almost unspeakable secret.

Despite her discomfort over that fact, Mom was Grandpa Joe's girl, raised as though she were his only child, and she hated leaving him most of all when, fourteen years old, she was sent back to her family. "She was very pretty," remembers Aunt Marge, "but she was odd."

***

Another telephone call from my mother pushes me to the edge of anguish. Already I want to unplug the phone, and even the thought of visiting her knots my stomach. Nonetheless, I answer and her voice is raw as a tent preacher's, not saying hello, but, "*Yeah.* I want my tablecloth back, the good one that was Uncle Arthur's. Jan *took* it. She *takes* all my stuff."

"We don't need your tablecloth, Mom. What's really wrong?"

"I couldn't sleep last night. I just worried and worried about my tablecloth. I'm worried *sick* about it."

I sense that she has indeed been lying awake nights constructing scenarios of her victimization, assembling disparate events, varied suspicions, a Winchester Mansion of odd and incongruent angles with her at their threatening nadir. For the past month, these pressures have collected, intensified, focused, and grown persistent.

At the core of it all, I have come to suspect, is the fact that Jan, my wife, has taken one thing of great consequence from Mom: her only child, me. Nothing I can say, however, persuades my mother of that. Every point I try to make is met by a nonsequitor.

"Jan sneaks in my house when I'm having my hair done," she asserts.

"She's teaching then, Mom."

"Her parents hung around bars."

"What's that got to do with it?" My tone is not kind.

"She wasn't raised with the Ten Commandments."

"What's that have to do with her sneaking into your place when she's teaching?" I ask.

"How do you *know* she's teaching?" she demands. "*You* aren't there."

Hurt but trying to point out the absurdity of her charges, I fire back, "They pay her to sneak into your house, then?"

"She was from a trashy part of town." Nonsequitors are limitless.

I sense that I'm making a mistake in responding to her accusations, a black hole sucking rationality from me. And I sense that something is deeply, deeply awry.

"She's taken all my stuff. I can't find *anything*." In fact, our kids and I — Jan by now stays away — usually find "stolen" articles without difficulty in my mother's mobile home. "*She* put it there," Mom accuses. "*I* certainly didn't. *I* didn't get to put my own stuff *anywhere*."

There is painful truth in her complaint. What actually occurred is that after Mom suffered a serious stroke late in 1986, I hired movers to pack my parents' belonging and transport them from Oildale to Petaluma; Pop's health was even worse than hers, so neither of them was well enough to help. In Petaluma, Mom underwent immediate and successful carotid artery surgery, so she could not begin to unpack her personal belongings until much later.

After forty-four years in Oildale, the move was a terrible dislocation for my parents, even though they had previously purchased their mobile home, ostensibly planning to join us soon. By the time they actually relocated, neither could drive a car or even write a check. I had to take charge of matters, including the painful sale of the house in which I had been raised. It was a grim time for all.

Now, however, the conviction that she was shanghaied to Petaluma has grown in my mother's mind. Her voice on the telephone grows more rapid, edging toward hysteria. "At *home* I knew where everything was," she says, then one of those radical changes of subject occurs. "*My* mother didn't let *me* stay out till all hours. *Someone* has been putting green rubber bands on my letters. *Someone* keeps going through my drawers."

When we eventually began to unpack their belongings, my ill and upset mother had sought to purge herself — "You take it. I don't want it. I don't care anymore." Jan and I had stored various of Mom's possessions, confident that her spirits would eventually rise. Now, not even remembering events of that time, she is obsessed by objects — those dishtowels ("They were *good* ones."), that steam iron ("It was a *good* one."), this sewing basket ("a *good* one"), many of them gifts never used. They have become powerful symbols of all Mom has lost as a result of age and infirmity.

"*Somebody* sneaks in while I'm sleeping," she cries, "and *moves* my things."

"Calm down," I urge, fighting frustration bordering on rage that surges within me. Anything wrong is my wife's fault, even though Jan left her teaching position for a year to help my parents while they were too ill to care for themselves, buying their groceries, paying their bills, transporting them on countless trips to doctors, all of this with only rare thanks from my sullen mother. Pop, on the other hand, has grown closer and closer to his daughter-in-law during his illness — they are now great and special pals — another possible source of my mother's seething.

"You won't *listen* to me!" hisses my mother.

"Have you been taking your medicine?" I finally demand.

"You think *I'm* loony," her voice fills with sobs, "but *she* is. She steals my stuff. She *hid* my chocolates. Those kids of yours stay out too late — *I* wasn't raised that way."

I almost lose control but take a deep breath, then ask, "Why don't you take your anti-depressant?"

"It's the bunk," she snaps, sobs suddenly gone.

As a child I was allergic to aspirin. According to my parents, I would run terrified through the house after taking one, shivering and babbling incoherently. My own recollection of those events is of being inhabited by an inchoate, overwhelming dread I could not escape. Could the same sort of thing be happening to my mother? I can't believe that the woman I have known for fifty years is truly this mean-spirited. It often feels as though she wants us punished because she is old, yet I know that can't be true. It is deeper, more ominous.

In frustration, I call her sister in Oregon, and she commiserates. "Sis can be a real downer at times. She had that breakdown when you were little," adds my aunt. I ask her more about it, but she has little to add. The specifics are mysterious to her.

In fact, I don't know for certain what that abstract word, "breakdown," actually means. I do know that Mom no longer makes sense. I am beginning to grasp that I have not seen these events for what they are — no, I am far too close, part of the problem, myself, so I haven't put things together.

The next day I take a deep breath then call Mom and ask about her earlier problem. Fortunately, it is one of her good days and she answers frankly: "You were little and I had that nervous breakdown. It was a long time ago. I had those shock treatments."

For a moment I say nothing. *Shock treatments.* This is new and utterly unexpected information, and I infer that such drastic therapy was hardly standard for what Mom calls "nerves." This is a loose thread in the emotional knot that has increasingly bound me.

As we continue talking, bits and pieces from that period come back to me: a trip to Southern California to pick Mom up, sitting in the Ford's front seat with my father, windows open, as we drove over the Grapevine from Oildale. I remember a large building and verdant grounds; I remember, too, the kind people who greeted us. Most of all, however, I remember how delighted I had been to see my mother again. My life was at that point still so immersed in hers that I was hardly a separate being.

I recall those things clearly, but the specifics — *why* she was there at all — had never been revealed. She later referred to the place as a rest home on those rare occasions when it was mentioned at all so, as a kid, I assumed she had simply rested.

"It was just nerves," she adds. But I am still thinking about shock treatments, because they at last may provide an unhappy perspective on the months of accusations, of dark suspicions, of outraged pleas from a woman normally good-natured if introverted.

Before her stroke, she had built a safe world for herself in Oildale where, despite agoraphobia, she was popular with her neighbors. Her grandchildren, for good reason, loved her deeply. But as they grew older, they sensed that she was *strange* — their word — given to powerful, apparently irrational likes and dislikes of things or folks with which or whom she had little or no experience.

The morning when she revealed her shock treatments, many things suddenly focused for me. Her dismal outlook, exacerbated by recent events, no longer seemed merely ugly, and her persistent claim of being a victim while she victimized someone else took on a new, deeper dimension. At that moment I recalled how she had once attacked the spouses of her brother and sister, and even of her aunts and uncles; in-laws consistently fared poorly in her world. Hearing her stories about them as a kid, I had simply assumed that they were a sorry lot, although all of them seemed fine to me.

When I am enduring those irrational calls, truth has remained her persistent, her frenzied claim: *"I don't lie."* She does indeed tell the truth as she knows it, or creates it, I now understand. Impossible charges are absolutely real to her.

It may or may not be psychosis, I realize, but it certainly is madness — a contagious and insidious condition that throws everyone it touches out of kilter. And I realize my own madness for not recognizing it. The buffeting has me, too, slipping toward strange fears and irrational rages, helplessly suspended between two women I love, one attacking the other.

That morning I talk with her physician and he, hearing my summary of her history of such behavior, says, "It sounds a great deal like paranoid depression. I should see her right away. If it's what it sounds like, it's chronic but controllable," he adds.

After seeing her, he tells me, "Sometimes with older people, symptoms of mental illness are passed off as senility or just the results of aging. But that's wrong. It's an illness and we can help her. No one is suffering more than your mother right now." He refers her to a psychiatrist and, two days later, she has her first session with him, emerging relaxed, perhaps purged. She begins taking a new, more effective medication that evening.

The results seem miraculous. A few days later she begins the course of drugs, and two of my sons ask, almost in tandem, "What's happened to Grandma? It's fun to go over there again." The following Sunday I take her to Mass. Afterward, we stop at a nearby grocery store as usual where, seeing the decorations, Mom says, "It's almost Easter," and shakes her head. After a moment, she stops, gazes at me, then adds with sudden concern in her voice, "Oh, I forgot Jan's birthday."

***

Raised as a first-generation immigrant child, Mom must have seemed strange indeed to brothers and sisters who were very much Americans. Although she had an older brother, Mom was placed in charge of the other children when her parents worked at various jobs, and her sister remembers her as a taskmistress.

Over the years tales have unfolded, often with laughter: the uncle who was separated from the family during the 1906 earthquake in San Francisco and ended up on an Alaskan fishing boat for three years; the versatile musicians and easy womanizers in her father's clan; the prepubescent sister who smeared lipstick on her face and flirted with truck drivers in a family-owned cafe. Now, however, dark memories dominate; we have been victimized, victimized: "Just our Johnson luck," she clucks.

Between less and less common glimpses of the pleasant woman I once knew, great engulfing silences open like the drift between continents, and none of us can easily penetrate them. There are slack starings, stunned eyes. Old age has not been kind to her. In fact, life has not been kind for it turns out that she possesses scant emotional margin to absorb its blows and shocks: the death of one brother fifty years ago, for example, still brings quick tears to her eyes as it always has, and she seems unable to escape the certainty that nearly everything after adolescence, especially marriage, has betrayed her dreams, just as she assumes that all her relatives have been victimized by unworthy mates.

My father was Mr. Everything in high school — handsome, student-body president, possibly the finest athlete in the town's history — and later a hail fellow well met, but he was not much of a husband. His own unhappy childhood simply didn't prepare him to give her the affection and support she so desperately needed. In retrospect, my parents are each fine individuals but they seem profoundly mismated. Mom was poorly prepared for harsh realities of an adversarial marriage and Pop, an excellent provider, was long on harsh realities.

As I grew up I observed, but did not understand, my mother's growing attempts to avoid the unavoidable, the breakdown she suffered, recovered from, then drifted toward again, and her slow journey into agoraphobia. Only family and close friends were sanctuaries, but not all of them. There were, after I married and left home, long stretches of depression with occasional severe dips, lengthy periods when she felt her life was sliding out of control. My children became her focus and she zeroed in on two of them in particular as something like perfect specimens, angrily rejecting any references to their shortcomings. She also convinced herself that my choice of a wife had been a tragic mistake and she hinted darkly from 300 miles south that I was being cuckolded.

When, twenty years into our marriage and after having raised five children, Jan at my urging returned to college, finished her degree and embarked on a career, it was clear evidence to my mother that my wife did not have a true commitment to being a wife: "She's not a good housekeeper." About that time, some of my kids' adolescent antics humanized them and Mom was distraught; they weren't perfect after all. Things were once more spinning out of control in her life.

Three years ago, she and my father — he in his last cogent days before multiple infarct dementia stole his mind — purchased a mobile home in a park a couple of miles from where Jan and I live, but they delayed moving into it, delayed until a year later when they were both so ill they could not care for themselves. The loss of her home has been at least as traumatic as the stroke itself.

It is a no-win situation for her and for me, because she initiates nothing. Her strategy is to beg for help then, once it is given, to complain in weak, injured tones about flaws: I moved her. I sold her house. I changed doctors for her and the new one does not offer carte-blanche pills. In doing those things, I have destroyed her world and, to a degree, my own.

"Why do things have to change?" she moans.

It is a constant plaint and, exhausted, I can mumble only, "That's life, Mom."

"Sure," she snorts, "nobody moved *you* from your home." She reaches into my belly and grabs my umbilical cord.

"Not yet, at least," I reply.

My mother has forgotten and now denies the first conversation we had after her stroke. My family and I had been camping in the Sierra when she was stricken and learned about it when we returned. I telephoned my folks upon returning to check in and a faint voice cried, "Where were you when I needed you?" I was stunned, not knowing what was wrong. When I tried to pry facts from her, they were not forthcoming. She had not yet seen a doctor, but a neighbor lady, one whose hypochondria led her to informally practice medicine, had informed mother that she'd suffered a "T.I.A." and that became Revealed Truth, that and the fact that I'd abandoned her.

I hurried to Oildale and took charge, scheduled appointments, ferried my mother on a round of medical visits, and learned not only that she had suffered not a T.I.A. but a complete stroke, but also that she required immediate carotid artery surgery. At that point I moved Pop and her to the mobile home they already owned.

Memories, Memories...

I was fourteen, playing football in high school and increasingly independent. Modeling myself after my tough-guy father, I now avoided mushy stuff, even in private.

Following my first week of preseason practice in Bakersfield's heat, I was still in bed on Saturday, luxuriating that easy morning, when I heard voices in the hall, then the door to my bedroom cracked open, and I knew my folks were gazing at me like proud parents studying their baby, so I kept my eyes closed, feigning sleep.

After a moment Mom said to Pop, "Look at Gerry's burr haircut. He looks like a little boy again."

"He's growing up," Pop replied, pleased that I had made the team.

I don't recall that my mother said anything, but she approached my bed, rubbed my bristly head and kissed my cheek. I kept my eyes closed, and I loved it.

There were few if any such displays later, but that one remains fresh in my mind today, nearly forty years later. In retrospect it seems that as my own rough male sexuality emerged, Mom's ability to show love for me seemed to diminish. I liked girls and was curious about sex, but was constantly encumbered by pronouncements like "I know you and _____ would *never* do anything to make me ashamed." Oh yes we would, not to make her ashamed, of course, but we'd do things; Mom didn't figure into our motives at all, but we certainly figured into hers. "My brothers would *never* do anything with girls that would hurt *their* mother." I'll bet. They, like me, had been boys, after all, not abnormally licentious, but boys. Nonetheless, those declarations burdened me with guilt.

During my high school years Mom fought her most valiant struggle against the fear that always hovered just ahead of her. Energized by my own activities at that time, she was able to leave the house with some frequency, attend a few meetings. She even joined the parents' club and the altar society in our parish church. She was especially supportive of academic and social lives, all but ignoring my athletic activities. I, of course, was most interested in sports.

Her concern and naiveté were endearing, and it was then I began to realize how sheltered she had been. Once she mentioned to the principal of the Catholic high school I attended that she thought it would be best if I wasn't allowed to participate in sports in order to channel all my energy into "more serious" pursuits. He had gently explained that young men like me, with their sap rising, needed physical activity. "I felt so dumb," she years later candidly acknowledged. "I never thought about kids thinking about sex being normal. And to cause *Brother*" — she intoned the word — "to talk about it...," she shook her head.

Her advice during those years was revealing but not consistently valuable. "Enjoy yourself," she cautioned, "these will be the best years of your life"; not so, but she believed it. When at seventeen I fell in youthful love, she told me that it would be my one and only true romance; not so, but she believed it. During those years, our lives — once so entwined that I felt I existed only in her love — were already unraveling. I caught her with her ear pressed to a door eavesdropping on one of my telephone conversations and angrily rebuffed her. Today I consider the episode funny — her nosiness no more irrational than my indignation. She still speaks of those days with some ambiguity — always whispering, never saying aloud even when we are alone, the name of that high-school girlfriend — an incantation for her version of my lost youth. When she hears my old chums and I reminisce over teenage adventures, there is often genuine shock in her eyes: you boys did that?

Memories, Memories . . .

> *"I'm so terribly ashamed," she wept, almost out of control, confronting me. Although she has never explained what triggered the outburst, I assume she had glimpsed me in a compromising position with a young woman.*
>
> *Well into my twenties, I had returned from the army and was living in a small apartment in the back of my folks' house while I saved money for college. I entertained there and, indeed, there were things to see if one wished to clandestinely observe some of those evening sessions.*
>
> *"I can't even walk in my own house," she sobbed.*
>
> *"Have you considered minding your own business," I snapped, angry and guilty. "If you snoop, you might not like what you find."*
>
> *"You weren't raised that way."*
>
> *"I wasn't raised at all." It was an injurious, thoughtless response and I later apologized, but our long simmering over different lives and values had finally flamed. I was an active young man with a young man's impulses; she was a reclusive middle-aged woman with her own notions. We harbored different illusions. It was time for me to depart for good before I destroyed what she had left of me. Shortly thereafter, I did just that.*

My father, unable to care for himself at all, resides with us now, as does my mother. Their relationship, never outwardly warm, is touching. He is slow but still recognizes her, and he often grins when I urge, "Give Mom a kiss," and she makes a face. At last, now that they have been battered by age and illness, it is possible for me to see an underlying need, perhaps the love, that once drove them. "My...little...bride," Pop stammers, his voice slowed and slurred,"...is...gonna...divorce...me."

At first she blinks, confused; he rarely manages complete sentences. Then she counters, "No, but I *should*, and take all your money."

He grins toothlessly. It is an intimate exchange, about as hot as they get.

Mom has never completely recovered from paranoid depression, but it has not become acute again. In retrospect, I realize that when her recent breakdown occurred, she had desperately needed her only child's attention, but my wife and I were then dealing with Pop's urgent needs plus the pressures of parenting, and were at first overwhelmed. I hadn't, and for awhile couldn't, imagine how disabled my father had become; although I was changing his diaper, I nonetheless found it difficult to grasp such sudden and radical reality.

Mom, meanwhile, floundered; she had lost not only her sparring partner of fifty-three years, but her son — the one who had been the focus of her life while that same father ignored him — suddenly seemed to care only for her undemonstrative husband. She could not realize that I had to build a bridge with my dad while I still could, and I did not then realize that I was contributing to her slow shattering. Now that her problem and my role in it has been diagnosed and dealt with, I am determined not to let her come apart again.

I recognize something now, or acknowledge it at last without embarrassment: our umbilical cord has never fully severed. As an adolescent and young man, this only child who had worshipped his mother veered sharply from her, battled — literally fought in some cases — to prove he wasn't a momma's boy. And I accomplished that, making the break as brutally clear as my much-shattered nose. But that cord still hangs there between Mom and me.

It is my turn to use it to protect her from the abyss of loneliness and fear yawning before her. I must be her lifeline and send love through that cord to her as certainly as she once pumped blood through it to me. My strategy is simple, the very one she had used on me when I was small and vulnerable: more hugs, more kisses, more tender tones to fight her demons — no matter how coldly such entreaties are received — because love is all that matters between us. But not merely between us, and this is a lesson she has taught me: in the final analysis, love is the affair of life, the central issue of our existence.

I kiss her, but she moves her face away from me, and my lips touch only the cold corner of her mouth. Mom looks at me then, her eyes wide and askew, her jaw jutting. "Somebody's been moving my teeth," she says.

COMING OF AGE IN CALIFORNIA

My mother was born in El Paso del Robles, California, my father in El Paso del Norte, Texas. Between these two passes exists a place or series of places, an idea or series of ideas, called *la frontera*...the frontier, the border, the edge.

My father's father's family moved west from upstate New York after having migrated from Wales, from England, from Scotland, and from Ireland. My mother's mother's family moved north from Mexico after having migrated from Spain, from Portugal, from Ireland, and likely from an Indian village somewhere.

I was born in *El Valle de los Tulares* — now called the San Joaquin Valley — of California, and my life has taken ethnic mixture a step further because I married a woman whose father is métis, a French and Cree combination originally from Canada, and whose mother is Polish and German. Our five children — all *gueros* — illustrate a variation of what Jose Vasconcellos called "*la raza cósmica*." We are southwesterners — El Paso and Paso Robles; we are Californians, dwelling *en la frontera*, on a cusp of cultures and races and perspectives.

No wonder the exuberant aroma of enchiladas always sweeps me back, back...my father, young then, his muscular brown arm bent out the car's window as he drove, my pretty mother smoking nervously and pleading, "Not so fast, Speck." We zoomed southwest from Oildale, through Taft and Maricopa, past wooden oil derricks and black reservoirs. From gradually rising land we could see a glistening incarnation of Buena Vista Lake below us if it was a wet year. Finally the car would climb out of the Valley into parched western mountains, toward the trickling Cuyama River with its wide canyon where snaky range cattle eyed our overheating chariot and where great condors soared while my father was pouring water from a canvas bag into the radiator.

24

I was a Valley boy, used to flat, apparently limitless vistas, so even the relatively unadorned landscape of the Cuyama with its mounted vaqueros, its sparse chaparral, its mysterious creases and arroyos, seemed exotic to me. Once in the late 1940s we met my mother's parents in the Cuyama and picnicked next to a lone, shady spring. My grandfather cut a green willow branch and laboriously made from it a whistle of the sort he had played with as a rural California boy long before plastic was invented. Grandpa was an avocational musician and he played a tune on the willow before handing it to me. Although I managed to coax no recognizable music from that whistle, and it eventually dried to a brittle twig, it remains one of three or four childhood treasures I have never forgotten.

Eventually Cuyama Canyon narrowed, steepened, and curve after tight curve carried us farther west. By then I was always vaguely carsick. Trees became more common, more varied, with Spanish moss draping many of them, until finally our auto at last emerged into a coastal valley, crossed one more sandy river, and arrived in Santa Maria. There, at my maternal Grandma and Grandpa's house, steaming platters of enchiladas — our holiday fare then as now — awaited us, and my carsickness quickly vanished.

I deliberately mention Grandma first; she was Ramona Silva, a third-generation Californian whose grandparents I earlier mentioned came north from Mexico. "Came from" is probably the wrong expression, for we never left: we lived in Hispanic America, *en la frontera* — as much frontier as border, and certainly never a barrier. In ways we did not even understand, we were border people because we were a family whose mixture foretold California's future. We recognized no clear limits between our nations or ourselves: "*En la frontera, son los mismos.*"

My grandfather, Jack Johnson, was of northern European descent, but his Latina wife's culture ruled this household as certainly as it had once ruled coastal California, and he gobbled those enchiladas as greedily as did his Spanish-speaking children; no sauerkraut for him. Theirs was a warm home, full of music and laughter but not much money; it was a place that I never ceased loving or looking forward to visiting. Even in

25

my teen years, I could quickly put aside adolescent rebellion to visit Grandma and Grandpa. In many ways that household now serves as a model for my own, right down to the enchiladas my non-Latin wife skillfully prepares, their intriguing smell merging joys and generations.

Today my clan retains the Hispanic concept of *la familia* and a fierce pride in that aspect of our heritage; it literally comes with the territory so it can sometimes be difficult for the deepest part of me to separate places from people. For example, my almost-*tia*, Alberta Garcia of the Santa Margarita Garcias; she and my uncle Dozy were engaged when he died suddenly in 1939, and forever after she was kin, as were her parents and siblings. Even her place, Santa Margarita, became our terrain. When we drove through it we knew we were home because the Garcias were there, and we had loved and grieved together.

It was unusual in Oildale — an all-white enclave then — for a youngster to have friends, let alone relatives, of as many varied colors as I did, and that fact worked to my advantage as I grew up and my world expanded. From the beginning, my California was composed of varied people. My father's friends included Billy Lee and Al Lum, progeny of pioneer Chinese families. For awhile he was employed by Jim and Mary Sandrini, who spoke rapid Italian but slow English; they remained close friends until their deaths and my hard-nosed father wept for them. More exotic to me were my first encounters with blacks in school sports and, while they seemed foreign indeed, I quickly learned that generalizations didn't apply because I met jerks and geniuses among them, just as I had among my own relatives. I worked with Filipinos in the grape fields near Cawelo and their physical variety amazed me — there were so many different *kinds*.

Something that didn't amaze me, however, was that I quickly landed a relatively soft job loading boxcars, while those darker, more experienced workers remained among the wasps and spiders and heat strokes in the fields. I understood even then the advantage my fair skin offered but was too complacent to stir up trouble by complaining. There was, you see, no perfection in my growing awareness: as a kid, I too told and laughed at Rastus-and-Liza jokes. I once referred to a Japanese-American friend as "One Hung Low," and only later did I realize how that sort of smug, smart-assed comment reflected the Yellow-Peril thought that encouraged an abomination like Executive Order 9066.

The important thing, I guess, is that I knew better even then — my family did not indulge in racism — but I found myself on occasion swept into the local habit of ignorant racial denigration. I have no excuse for my lapses. As luck would have it, when my parents sent me to junior high and high school in Bakersfield — "Oildale Okie" became my new nickname — my circle of friends quickly included more nonwhites than whites, so the tacitly encouraged social racism of Oildale faded fast. It was not possible to yearn for the beautiful Linda Lum or sneak a beer with rowdy Quincy Williams and at the same time indulge in racist generalizations. Nor was it possible to be called nigger lover with any frequency and not realize that no social ideal had been or would in the immediate future be achieved locally.

I early on came to believe with James Baldwin that "All men are brothers. That's the bottom line. If you can't take it from there, you can't take it at all." I chose to take it. A number of my closest white friends only tolerated my attitudes and I only tolerated theirs. It was certainly easier for me to ignore at least some racial stereotypes because by then I thought of myself as either an Okie or a Hispanic, I wasn't certain which.

That Latin spirit was not merely a matter of illusion, although it certainly was illusory. Like most American mongrels, any statements I make concerning ethnicity are symbolic; despite the large dose of northern European genetic material that courses my family's veins, we remain symbolically Hispanic, Spanish-speaking and are living in this erstwhile province of Spain and Mexico in no small measure because of the Latin matriarchy alluded to earlier.

My older daughter, Alex, and a boyfriend named Augustine Estrella, were at a college party not long ago when one coed began speaking disparagingly about "Spics." It was so anachronistic an attack that for a second no one objected, but then Alex — an athlete who is nothing if not tough — shook her

blonde head and said, "Hey watch your mouth, girl. *I'm* a
Spic." Augie, born in Mexico and a dimension darker, quickly
added, "Me, too."

The speaker was abashed and finally said, "Oh, I didn't
mean *you* guys," and wisely changed the subject.

But for me, older and mellower and considerably more
addled, my link to blood and land is confused with memories:
driving north from Santa Maria as a boy with my parents, we
would pass Nipomo and the truck farm of a man named Otoi,
a Japanese-American who had been hauled away to a reloca-
tion camp during World War II — "A buncha damn bullshit,"
said my father who had played football with Otoi — then we'd
pass Pismo and reach the barren coastal shelf that is now called
Shell Beach where I would be shown again the stand of trees
and old farm buildings that once were ours until somehow they
were lost to crooked bankers and lawyers early in this century,
or so the story goes.

Who lived there? Well, my great-grandmother, Esperanza
Terrill did. The rancher would have to have been John (or João)
Silva (or Silveira), my great-grandfather, although by the time I
heard the story, he was confused with Jose Castillo, Great-
grandma's second husband. In fact, poor Silva was and remains only the slimmest sliver of memory in our family, while
Castillo, with his handlebar mustache and Chihuahuan accent,
is uniformly adored. But Silva lives in my blood and he, like
that place, those coastal canyons and the barren bed of the
Cuyama River, is merged in my remembrance with the breath
of enchiladas: where does one end and the other begin?

The Shell Beach rancho was where my grandmother was
born, and Mom drew first breath in Paso Robles an hour or so
north — the same place as her own grandmother, aforementioned Esperanza. South, on a stream with a waterfall inland
from Arroyo Grande, is where Dozy and Alberta used to take
me fishing when I was little more than an infant; I still have a
fading photo taken of us there. Farther south, near Orcutt, my
Uncle Bus as a small boy was sneaking the pleasure of a barn-
yard leak in the presence of a large rooster and his pecker suddenly became the peckee — a story repeated with various em-
bellishments throughout my youth. It was a cautionary tale

but it didn't take; I was no more apt to keep my plumbing to myself than was any other lad.

We often drove home from Santa Maria the long way, north to Paso Robles, then east, again across the coastal hills, much lower and less green there, until we'd emerge near Lost Hills and the landscape would open into the treeless flatland that was my primary California. Early on I added the central coast to my version of the state and for many years that was it: one corridor from Oildale to Santa Maria to Paso Robles, and another from Oildale to Woodland in the Sacramento Valley — that was California.

Why Woodland? Well, while part of my father's family was also located in Santa Maria, there was no warmth in that setting. Fred Haslam, known to me as "Grandpa Fred," lived there with an unpopular stepmother. Pop's deepest familial passion was directed almost solely toward his mother who had died in the great flu epidemic of 1918, a mother he has to this day never ceased mourning. As a result, we frequently drove north toward the farm just outside Woodland where Marie Martin, my grandmother, had been born and where Aunt Jess and Uncle Henry then lived. Pop's older sister, Isabel, and her large brood dwelled in another family home in the town proper, so the seat of Yolo County was a location to which my father felt a link. Moreover, my grandmother was also buried there, so I could touch the granite tombstone my grieving grandfather had long ago purchased for his young wife.

Among my earliest recollections is of sitting on my mother's lap as we motored up Highway 99 in the Central Valley toward Yolo County and of thinking that things smelled funny once we left Oildale. I was so used to the sulfuric breath of crude oil that air without it seemed bland as lettuce. Ahead flatland stretched as far as I could see or dream: the air swerved with heat and a puddle of false water shimmered before us. On all sides I saw fields that disappeared into distant haze. There was no limit; physical space seemed to suck the imagination.

In those days, the trip north took us past citrus the size of family homes and signs announcing: "Only 5 miles to the BIG ORANGE. Fresh Squeezed Juice. Ice Cold. Radiator Water Free." "Only 3 miles to the BIG ORANGE..." My folks have acknowledged that those trips consisted of two litanies: "When're we gonna get there?" and "Can't we stop, Daddy, Pleeeeease?" There were other bold notices, too, exotic and much, much more titillating — "LIVE RATTLESNAKES! SCORPIONS! COLD BEER! GILA MONSTERS!" I don't remember us ever having stopped: "SEE A COBRA!"

When we crossed occasional streams in the valley, dark, slim forests decorated both sides of the water and stretched narrowly east and west of the highway as far as I could distinguish. Often an old car or two would be parked near the water in those days, and people with cane poles sat there fishing. Occasionally whole camps were assembled next to those streams, with families or groups of families living out of cars with tarps stretched between them or splotched canvas tents erected.

At long intervals across that great prairie, ranks of palm trees, like somnolent sentries, leaned along ranch roads. Those occasional ranches themselves usually appeared as no more than dark clusters of trees with perhaps a metal barn glinting in summer sun. It was not unusual to see a large dust plume where a tractor worked its way along a field or a spinning dust devil dancing madly over open tracts. A few years later, working in a nearby field, I would dash to the center of a whirlwind and stand, eyes squeezed shut and breath held tightly, while the funnel jolted my body and particles stung my skin.

I recall the communities we passed on Highway 99 as little more than lines of packing sheds — the highway paralleling the railroad tracks — with one or two perpendicular business streets, and groups of men huddled on corners. Cafes seemed to be surrounded by pick-up trucks, and well-dressed, unaggressive people stood on corners holding *Watchtowers*. There were many churches with cryptic signs: "The wages of sin is death" or "Jesus wept." Today Freeway 99 denies those vistas and communities are mere names on green signs hovering above you as you drive.

San Francisco was admitted to my version of the state after a visit with my great-grandmother, "Grandma Esperanza," who lived with her consort, Castillo, her two surviving sons, Joe and Tudy, plus their revolving girlfriends and unrevolving children, in a claustrophobic flat on outer Geary Street. The place smelled like an old closet and even now seems to me to have been not only bare of material and light, but of hope as well: people waiting to die. My initial impressions of that city were not flattering: too many people, too many hills, too much fog. I did not come to love it until years later when my young wife and I attended San Francisco State and lived in Gatorville, married students' housing on the edge of Lake Merced.

A couple of years after that initial visit to outer Geary, my dad took me to a UCLA-Nebraska football game in the Los Angeles Coliseum. During that two-man journey into the exotic Southland where air thickened, where strange flowers and cactus dotted hillsides, Pop recounted youthful experiences and pointed out locales, so I finally acknowledged the megalopolis that loomed beyond the Tehachapis: it too seemed hilly, but also dry and huge and somehow Arabic to me, strangely alluring.

Despite my small-town upbringing, I did not fall into the provincial trap that once claimed a friend who implied that only Malibu was California, that all the rest was purgatory. My version of the state continued growing and I soon realized that any homogeneous sense of this diverse series of places gathered under one name was chimerical. Here, as elsewhere, change is endemic, and new residents characterize and define many regions.

I eventually recognized that this state meant something quite different to many other people. To them, newcomers and outsiders mainly, California — or, rather, the idea of California — epitomized a flashy, traditionless, mobile future: a paradigm for the deconstruction of culture, old values and inhibitions flying away in all directions like the expanding universe. My California, on the other hand, was the place where I could visit my great-great-grandmother's grave and gaze on the same oaks she so admired; it is the place where I was conceived and where I would conceive my own children. For me, it was and remains as rooted and as real as flesh on flesh — an other, *the* other, California.

Only later did I recognize not only that those two Californias exist, but that the former version, Fantasy California I call it, was a product of the nation's core of power — the abstract, nondialect, nonplace that directs economic culture and much popular taste from an invisible nucleus often assumed to be vaguely "east"; my version of the state, no matter what its geographic reality, was from that perspective a mere region, outside the self-appointed hub, a margin of dialect and tradition and reality that didn't fit the needs or illusions of Fantasy California or of those who invented it. On the other hand, my region was (and is) an actuality, not a desire being acted out.

Reading native daughter Joan Didion's keen prose some years ago, I was at first befuddled by the persistent craving I sensed in her version of the Central Valley which, as it turned out, was anything but central to her aspirations. It took me awhile to realize that she and I may have been raised in that same great trench but most similarities ended there: her people were affluent, well-educated, socially prominent and she, of course, was a she — all distant from my experiences. But there was more: Didion really believed that she resided on a grim margin and she agonized over it — yearning, yearning, yearning for the cultural core, whether it be California's New York City or New York City's California.

She didn't recognize that the locus of literary power was tilting, slowly tilting, away from that phantom center toward the disparate places where Americans really live. America *is* Vermillion, South Dakota, *is* Fayetteville, Arkansas, *is* Moscow, Idaho and, yes, *is* Oildale, California...as well as but not instead of Manhattan, New York. What Didion sought was only the blue image from an old flash bulb, gone before she even yearned for it.

But I, a blue-collar bumpkin, thought Oildale with its racism and xenophobia and resistance to new ideas was fine, thanks. I thought that because I also knew its love and its courage and how it rewarded hard work. To me, more naive certainly, the nation like the state consisted of regions, and mine was simply one of them. I wasn't then, nor am I now, willing to concede power to anyone, although my years as a writer have convinced me of the clout in personal contacts ("So you're so-and-so's boy, are you?") and persistence of stereotypes (the cocaine mansions of Beverly Hills as California landscape).

In any case, Didion's variation was as unfamiliar and as intriguing to me as Chinua Achebe's Nigeria, yet some college colleagues were telling me that it was *the* contemporary Valley, *the* contemporary California, *the* contemporary world. I knew it to be *a* Valley, *a* California, *a* world — brilliantly if idiosyncratically presented. Not one of my relatives or acquaintances had ever expressed a concern over membership in the Pacific Union Club or distress over not being included in Southern California's high (or low) society. I *had* heard tense talk of irrigation allotments, of love affairs and social diseases, of fist fights and even books. "Working steady" was a sacred incantation. No one I knew ever said they yearned for San Francisco or any place else, except maybe Pismo Beach on a hot day.

Through the entire and continuing process of building my personal golden state — adding the Sierra, the Colorado desert, the Siskyous, the vast Mojave and more — the aroma of even lousy enchiladas could carry me over that Cuyama route to a real California where my impecunious grandfather would convert a chunk of juniper hedge into a Christmas tree finer than any I've ever bought, where first-person stories about Joaquin Murrieta were recounted ("Those rangers they never got him."), and where Uncle Bus's maimed anatomy somehow summarized life's verities.

Nonetheless, I must admit that the Great Central Valley not San Clemente or Pacific Heights remains California's apotheosis for me. It also verifies physics because now when I motor south from rural Sonoma County where we live, through endless space toward Oildale, I also travel in time: the sky is the same, the fields the same, the trees, even the aromas are the same if you escape the freeway, and my breath catches as I urge my car back to the spot that gave me life because something essential in me remains unchanged too.

I always expect to see Quincy Williams or Jimmy Agalos, Joe Copeland or Larry Austin, Wally Coleman or Leroy Daniels — all dead for decades — bounce up the street on sixteen-year-old legs, exchanging grins and small talk, a few wheezing laughs. We'd surely discuss girls — matrons now — and josh over ball games. Larry and Joe played on a junior high team at Emerson that had nipped my Garces squad 72-0, a score that remained an enduring joke between us. Those aforementioned girls figured in other contests, real or imagined apprentice sexual encounters, often as competitive as anything on the field and certainly more ambiguous.

Here, where both lust and love awakened in me, I am even today swept by urgent sensuality each time I visit: the *place* remains an erogenous zone. Some women I know are as young and alluring to me now as forty years ago. And, of course, I took the best of Oildale with me, Jan who remains the love of my life. I walk through Oildale and nearby Bakersfield a man unburdened but bifurcated, young and old, innocent and jaded, yet always refreshed and grateful for the place and for my life. While I don't reject Paris or Honolulu, I don't yearn for them either because this is my home, this is me. I must breathe here to know myself. This is where I began to build California and where I came of age. This is where age is coming for me.

Jan and I met Fred and Rachel Dominguez for dinner in Bakersfield to celebrate my fiftieth birthday. Fred — "Duke" to his friends — is *padrino* of our son Carlos and one of my boyhood buddies; he had been on the field when we threw that 0-72 scare into Emerson back in 1950. The four of us, along with another special friend, Tom Alexander, who was too smart to play football, savored enchanting aromas, rich flavors — not enchiladas, this time, but Basque food — and swapped stories.

Scion of a family of vaqueros, Duke is a virtuoso tale teller and that comfortable evening he once more regaled us:

"Twenty-five, maybe thirty years ago, when I was working in the post office in East Bakersfield, there was an old Irish vaquero who used to come in there named Justin Caire. He'd ridden with my father and grandfather on the Tejon. Anyway, one day near Christmas he came in holding something behind his back and said, `Dominguez, I want you to have this,' and he handed me a beautiful inlaid silver bit made by Dan Garcia in Santa Margarita. I was shocked because I hardly knew him, and I said, 'Are you sure you want to give me this, Mr. Caire?'

"He looked at me and said that when he was a kid and just breaking in as a buckaroo, my grandfather was his foreman. One day he'd mentioned to Grampa how much he admired his bit. Well, Grampa just climbed off his horse, removed the bit and handed it to Mr. Caire. When he'd said that it was too valuable to accept, Grampa told him, 'No, you're my friend, my *compañero*, and what's mine is yours. It's the California way.' Mr. Caire said it was a lesson he'd never forgotten, and now he was giving it back to me fifty years later because, although he barely knew me, he knew I was a Dominguez and that I'd appreciate it."

Jan, who has heard my own family's stories for more than a quarter century, reached over and squeezed my hand because she knew we had come full circle, romance and reality: my own great-great-grandfather had been an Irish vaquero on the Tejon in 1860. And I, a man whose dreams have in large measure come true, surrounded by people I love in a place I love, could only grin.

REFLECTIONS FROM AN
IRRIGATION DITCH

That day the water ran crystalline between the rows of potatoes. My bare feet were sunken in one channel's soft bottom between furrows while that cool, clear current pulled brown smoke from them, flowing parallel to other mini-streams toward a far, perpendicular ditch that would catch the runoff we called "tailwater" and channel it along the county road toward a reservoir at the property's corner. I was eight years old then, and I pretended those artificial currents were racing, choosing a favorite — the one already ahead — and urging it toward distant victory, then exulting.

My Uncle Pete straddled a row next to me, a shovel leaning against one shoulder, his feet planted in two streams. He reached down and pulled a young potato from the earth, washed it in the clear flow, then opened his pocket knife and sliced me a sample. "Try it, Gerry," he urged. "It's sweet as all getout."

We were standing only a short mile from where the foothills of the Tehachapi mountains began sealing the southern end of California's Great Central Valley, near the point where desiccated Caliente Creek slipped from the high country to curl around those same foothills and to fade almost unnoticed onto cultivated land, and where it still occasionally and unpredictably reminded farmers of its existence with a stunning spring flood. West of us, the apparently flat terrain gradually, ever so gradually, sloped — agricultural patch after agricultural patch — until it was lost in shimmering heat waves that hid distant Bakersfield.

I accepted the proffered piece a little reluctantly — it might be a trick, since my uncle had already begun initiating me into the rough world of masculine joshing. Finally I bit into it and immediately made a face. To my palate, spoiled by Saturday-matinee candy, the potato-sliver tasted starchy and bland.

"What's wrong?" he asked.

"It tastes crappy." Toleration of such mild profanity was another aspect of our growing male camaraderie.

My uncle's lined, leathery face smiled then, and he popped a thick slice into his own mouth and crunched it. "You'll learn," he said. "There's nothing better than something fresh out of the ground. Nothing better." He was not an especially articulate man, but on this subject his words were unambiguous and as clear as the water in which we stood.

He knew the soil, Uncle Pete did, its tastes and its smells, for he had been raised on a farm near Shafter and had earned his living as a field foreman for various spreads in Kern County. The land here was too expensive to ever allow him to acquire a place of his own, a frustration that led him to try other work but to always return to farming, to always remain close to the earth even if it belonged to someone else.

When, many years later, a severe stroke felled him and my uncle was consigned to a chair in a room in a house in a city, yearning, ever yearning, for the open country and open life he so loved, I came to understand how sweet that potato had tasted. The final time I saw him, after another devastating stroke left him connected to tubes and machines in the intensive-care unit at Memorial Hospital in Bakersfield, his consciousness supposedly blasted, his eyes nonetheless followed me with torturous certainty — my uncle was in there, lurking. By then I had grown, and that long-ago slice, that crystal water, and that rugged and imperfect man, had become as precious as breath itself. Too late. Too late.

A couple of years after sampling potato from my uncle's knife blade, I wore something irreplaceable into an irrigation ditch just across the field. My mother treasured her high school class ring, cherished it more than I could imagine. Many years later in a repeated, sadly revealing series of episodes, she would tell each of my children to enjoy high school because those would be the best years of their lives.

But I knew nothing of that when I begged, cajoled, whined, pleaded — used every persuasive trick in my only child's repertoire — until she reluctantly agreed to allow me to don her ring, a twist of tape at the back of my finger to secure it, an admonition twisted into the back of my mind, *"Don't you lose it!"*

For awhile — a day or two, maybe a week — I treated that ring, that finger, that hand, like the Gifts of the Magi, protecting them in a pocket when I walked, removing them only to thrust into the faces of startled acquaintances — "It's *real* gold!"

That following weekend, however, back out at the ranch, I was romping with my cousin in an irrigation ditch, pretending we were professional wrestlers — a new fascination — bouncing, battering, splashing and wallowing, a good, old-fashioned romp. Eventually, we were called in for lunch, so after hosing mud from ourselves we walked to the yard where sandwiches and lemonade awaited us in comforting shade.

I had just seated myself at the picnic table when I heard those words: "I hope you didn't lose my ring with all that roughhousing." In a moment that remains slow-motion and precise now, over forty years later, I glanced down at my bare finger, then came as close to swooning as I ever would.

I don't recall exactly what happened to the sandwich or the lemonade, but we — my mother, my cousin, my aunt, and me —spent most of the afternoon in that well-churned ditch. Later my uncle and a couple of field workers joined us, but we found nothing. The ring was lost.

I was not punished, not physically anyway. My mother was too devastated to do more than gaze at me and moan, "I *begged* you not to wear my ring." She remained strong enough to physically restrain my father, but considerable time was to pass before I felt the shadow of that lost keepsake fade from our immediate relationship. On a deeper level, it never has, for at certain sad times even today, she reminds me of it.

But I managed to put things into perspective when I was seventeen because of two events. The first was an occurrence worthy of *Ripley's Believe It Or Not:* I came in from a day of maneuvering a tractor over a distant field and found Aunt Marge and Uncle Pete examining something at the kitchen table. My uncle had been plowing the field just behind the barn and had hit an old irrigation casing. When he'd climbed from his big, yellow Caterpillar to pull cement shards from the earth, he had noticed a small, black lump: Mom's ring. Unfortunately, even after being cleaned up, it bore only faint resemblance to her golden memory, but at least it had reappeared — the consequence of hundreds of candles lit for St. Anthony, Mom later claimed.

That same summer, a girlfriend lost my high school class ring while water skiing. She climbed into the boat after a spill, realized it was gone, then began weeping softly. I was afraid she had been hurt and was relieved to learn she was okay; the ring's loss troubled me but not deeply. I certainly didn't want it lost, but there was nothing I could do about that. I did, however, worry about telling my mother. Eventually I was deprived of that girlfriend too, by the way — a far more painful and consequential experience.

Mom was predictably upset over the loss of my ring, and she built pagodas of melted wax but this time St. Anthony was otherwise occupied. For myself, I had already determined that high school was no more than an early station on a much longer journey. Mom, who had matured during the Great Depression, had enjoyed few of the abundant opportunities my generation took for granted, so when I'd lost her ring in that ditch, I'd also displaced her dreams and a small token of her worth. My own ring was no such talisman for me.

There was a time, however, when I certainly could have used a charm. At twenty-one, I was floundering, having lost the aforementioned girlfriend and having flunked out of college, both by dint of profound immaturity. There had been other girls then, too many of them really, and I had met but did not then date the one who would eventually be my wife. Just as well that she and I didn't grow close during that pained period, for my life was swerving without focus. Childish illusions that had previously sustained me had blown away like Valley fog, and I found myself back at an irrigation ditch with Uncle Pete.

He employed me to dip, slice, and plant seed potatoes. I also watered twenty-five acres of sugar beets and eighty more of barley, did some discing, some plowing. I planted many personal seeds, too. One shirtless afternoon, for instance, straddling a vat of corrosive sublimate solution while pulling sacks of soaking seed-potatoes from it, I slipped and was immersed. Fifteen years later, a surgeon would carve a black lesion from my chest, identify it as cancer, and tell me that I was lucky indeed that it had been removed so early. We talked about what might have caused it, and I remembered that sun, that vat, that youthful invincibility — all unarguably gone.

My habit of working shirtless indirectly led to an episode that Uncle Pete never forgot. We often rattled our pickup after work to a beer bar called The Buckhorn. One early summer evening, we were guzzling brew with other farmers when a woman who looked like she had gone two falls with the Masked Marvel slid into the group, slapping backs and laughing in a voice that could remove warts.

Uncle Pete was a good-looking man, and the formidable lady paid him increasingly serious attention. He did not act especially interested, but did seem to enjoy kidding her. Finally, she said that she'd like to take a ride with him to see the farm where he worked — this long after dark. He winked at me, then said, "If you do, you'll have to dress the way Gerry does — no shoes, no socks, and bare to the waist."

For a minute she posed expressionless, then smiled. "Well, I just *might*," she said, and she reached down and removed one large shoe.

"Time for us to hit the road," my uncle said, the hint of an edge in his voice.

I was halfway through a draft beer and feeling no pain, so I hesitated, but he wasn't kidding. I hurried after him, that woman's excoriating laughter in the background. Once in the truck, I asked why we'd left so suddenly.

He grinned. "Two more minutes and that honky-tonk heifer woulda been buck naked. No thanks." Time passed and the woman grew larger and homelier, her clothing scantier and her ambitions ever more prurient as the anecdote was told and retold. At the time, it had seemed an event of small moment, but twenty years later it had become legendary.

In truth, there were few laughs during that stay on the farm, but those long days alone in the fields, those hours directing water, shoring up ditches, and those nights of exhausted, easy sleep were what I needed. Eventually, I decided to volunteer for the army, an experience that would abolish the final vestiges of my childish delusions and help me gain perspective. After a couple of years I returned home, discharge papers in my pocket, determined to complete college and to write.

Many years later, marriage and career in full flower, I drove my family by the ranch where my aunt and uncle had lived and worked in the open country near Arvin. It was a hot, late-summer day with a mirage floating ahead on the blacktop, and I stopped our car on the county road marking the western boundary of the field where I had once yearned to be someone else somewhere else. Across the dusty green of unripe cotton, I saw the old house shimmering, the barns, the water tank, plus a scattering of dark trees and, well behind them, dehydrated hills where we had hunted. There was a man shimmering in heat waves far off across the tract, wraithlike. He was irrigating, most likely. He did not look familiar but his job did.

At twelve I had chopped cotton in this very field, my first grown-up job, and I wanted to tell my kids about it, to give them a potato slice, but this fevered view was all there was. I remained uncharacteristically mute.

"Let's go, Daddy," urged Alexandra. "It's hot."

"That's where I worked when I was little."

"It's hot, Dad," Fred said.

"Yeah," I agreed, "it is." They had never chopped cotton and never would if I could help it. But I had. I started the car and, after one more longing look, drove away.

BROTHERS' BOY

Richard Rodriguez and I were talking one morning prior to taping an interview at Western Public Radio's studios in San Francisco when he casually said, "I went to Christian Brothers' High School in Sacramento."

I couldn't help grinning. "No kidding. I graduated from Garces Memorial in Bakersfield."

"Ah, so you're a Brothers' Boy too," he nodded, his smile broadening.

Leo Lee, the program's producer, who had been adjusting equipment in the studio while Richard and I chatted, overheard us, straightened up, then he too grinned: "I don't want to shock you two, but I went to St. Mary's Prep in Berkeley." So he also had been educated by the Christian Brothers.

That unexpected coincidence immediately changed our relationship because being a Brothers' Boy is one of those special categories of experience that does not fade, that brings with it a range of shared experiences and of pride. Like being a Marine or a mother, it sticks.

The Institute of the Brothers of the Christian Schools, called the Christian Brothers, was founded in 1680 by St. John Baptist de La Salle in Reims, France. The distinct white collar and black robe that is their uniform dates to that time. Not until 1819 in Ste. Genevieve, Missouri, did a community of Brothers begin teaching in the United States. When I entered Garces in 1949, the order taught in secondary schools all over California; Cathedral in Los Angeles, San Joaquin Memorial in Fresno, and Sacred Heart in San Francisco were especially well-known.

Today, I consider the decision that sent me to Garces to have been among the most important of my life. I had by no means been a juvenile delinquent in public school, but I was — as a note from my sixth-grade teacher revealed — "a disruptive under-achiever." After I had visited the principal's office a couple of times, endured swats, and had barely passed the sixth grade at public school in Oildale, it was decided that I should be sent to the Catholic institution in nearby Bakersfield. This was no insignificant verdict for my parents, since it involved economic hardship and personal inconvenience. To me, it was a novel idea I did not resist.

As a result, I encountered the black robe and white collar draped on the red-faced, imposing form of a middle-aged man named Brother Gerald. He was my first male teacher and, a couple of weeks into the seventh grade, I observed a scholar named Schaefer snap a disrespectful remark at Brother Gerald, then turn and smirk at the rest of us. A moment later, Schaefer was yanked from his seat, slapped, and thrust back into his seat in such rapid order that I wasn't certain it had really occurred although the whimpering miscreant harbored no doubts about it. He had not been sent to the office; his parents were not called; the school psychologist was not consulted. No, summary justice was administered, then Schaefer was publicly asked if he understood that such nonsense would not be tolerated. He did.

And he wasn't the only one. I had just been loosening up at that time, beginning to entertain my new classmates as I had my old ones, but that spectacle of quick and certain punishment prompted me to put my showbiz career on hold. Old habits die hard, however, and when a robin flew into our classroom through an open window a couple of weeks later, I could not resist and launched into an athletic imitation of the confused bird.

Too soon the great dark shadow of Brother Gerald loomed over me, and I found myself briskly escorted to the front of the class. As I made that gallows' walk, visions of Schaefer danced through my head. The executioner, however, merely tapped my trembling palm with a linoleum paddle and said, "Just remember that this is only a sample. Don't make me do this again. Now take your seat and keep quiet." It was a laying on of hands worthy of Oral Roberts because I was healed, no longer a discipline problem. The devil had been exorcised.

As it turned out, the only acceptable way to attract attention in Brother Gerald's class was through academic effort, a message that most of us eventually understood, some more reluctantly than others. Once an unexceptional scholar with whom I played football had to repeat nearly all his academic courses, so he was a year older than his classmates. He became famous for cadging homework from younger, smaller boys — some of whom developed the habit of doing theirs in duplicate. Once the Brothers suspected that something was amiss, however, he also became the only lad *always* called upon to explain his answers at the blackboard, where he *always* imitated a beached catfish.

My first days of Catholic education were somewhat trying because entering junior high can be tough even without changing schools and towns. A friend had entered Garces the year before and he had offered advice *via negative:* "A big mouth like you, everyone's gonna kick your butt." As it turned out, he was almost correct. But that wasn't entirely bad, since we quickly shook out my spot in the school's pecking order. Fighting actually seemed to be tolerated within limits by the faculty. Those boundaries included not allowing anyone to be bullied into a clash, quickly stopping one-sided battles, and carefully monitoring conflicts to make certain no one was injured. It seemed an eminently sensible approach to me, instructional in itself.

Even the student population of my new class proved to be an education, I soon discovered. In Oildale, everyone had been white, and was what today would be called working class, since nearly everyone's parents had toiled in the nearby oilfields. All my classmates at Standard School had been versions of myself. Garces, on the other hand, attracted a heterogeneous population from all over Kern County: rich and poor, white and non-white, Catholic and non-Catholic. Spanish, though discouraged except in the class of the same name, was frequently heard and my first and enduring friends there were other social outsiders, Mexican-Americans principally. Having learned some Spanish at home was a great help to me. Through it all, the Brothers seemed to be remarkably even-handed, rewarding work, punishing sloth, ignoring other considerations.

Sports were viewed not as distractions, but as integral parts of the educational mission at Garces. The Brothers, males struggling with celibacy themselves, understood full well the titillation of adolescent sexuality, so they promoted vigorous exercise. My dad said they were "channeling the sap."

It was difficult *not* to compete in athletics. This general participation, not the apocryphal reports of recruiting I heard discussed by friends at public schools, was the reason we were able to compete effectively against public schools with much larger student populations. We won California Interscholastic Federation championships in both football and basketball during my tenure. The Brothers also extolled the self-discipline and teamwork athletics promoted. A high percentage of the student body participated in more than one sport.

While in junior high school, I became immediately aware of social castes and realized that they were weightier than racial categories. In the seventh grade, for the first time in my life, I was subjected to condescension by children of wealth, most of whom I considered jerks. It was frustrating because normal remedies did not apply: punching them out, earning better grades, consigning them to the bench in sports — nothing seemed to weaken the mind-set that assigned me an intrinsically inferior status: I still lived in Oildale and they still lived in La Cresta; I summered at a packing shed, they summered at a country club.

In the long run, though, rich kids turned out to be good guys who, like me, had social lessons to learn. By the time we were high school seniors most of them had come to understand that affluence was not the only or most important thing you might have in common with others, and some of them "dated down," even interracially.

In fact, interracial everything was common among all but the most socially isolated at Garces and I learned early that a brown fist on my snout felt no better than a white one. While the Brothers were unquestionably aware of the social distinctions and churning, and certainly courted financial support from high-rollers, no sense of elitism crept into the classroom.

The social situation at Garces was somewhat atypical of Brothers' institutions, I have learned, because it was the only Catholic high school in the county. Elsewhere, the Christian Brothers specialized in educating boys from blue-collar families — to do so was a tenet of St. John Baptist de la Salle when

he founded the order principally to educate impoverished youngsters in France, a novel idea indeed in the seventeenth century. Elsewhere, the Christian Brothers are still said to provide the Church's working-class education (while the Jesuits,
for example, are reputed to offer a white-collar version). Also,
unlike most other schools run by the Brothers, there were girls
at Garces, though not in our classes; no, they were confined to
their own section of campus and instructed by Dominican nuns.

Boys and girls ate lunch together, participated in extra-
curricular functions — yearbook, forensics, rallies — and dated
on weekends, but our classrooms were male enclaves. Not
surprisingly, they secretly housed some crude diversions, especially toward the back of the room where less-dedicated schol-
ars like me tended to gather: farting was a popular pastime,
for example, and lighting farts during slide shows or movies
was considered a great adventure indeed. One future business impresario became famous for causing chaos by exposing
a certain prominent feature of his anatomy at unlikely times.

John Renfree, then a football stalwart, now a physician,
who sat in the front of the class by the way, grins and says,
"That was no-man's land back there, rank city. But it could
sure calm down in a hurry when Coach Dugger cruised
through." Ah, yes, Tom Dugger: a lay teacher as well as a
football coach, and a good man, who once in response to an
error in judgment on my part lifted me, desk and all, then sent
me — an experimental aircraft — toward distant climes. After
that I decided to use study hall to study.

In any case, the majority of students at Garces did not
engage in back-of-the-classroom displays. A certain burden of
familial ambition drove us; our parents hoped we would ride
education toward broader opportunities than they had enjoyed,
and a significant number of us have indeed taken advantage
of the education provided by the Brothers to achieve satisfying
professions and lives.

Academic demands at Garces were democratic and relent-
less but also charitably realistic. I particularly recall the Brothers insisting that the world was not an easy place, but that
work and work alone might allow us to prevail in it. Says
Justin Meyer of Silver Oak Cellars, another football player, whose

father was a railroad laborer, "What really happened is that they made it possible for us to dream of being things our folks couldn't even imagine. When that happened, it was up to us to succeed." Not making an honest effort at things seemed to be the great sin.

Recently, I read Wilfred Sheed's observation that "more kids come to hate the Church through its schools than through anything else that happens to them...they're not going to pick up any religious instruction that's worth much anyway at that age." By high school, I had come to distinguish between two distinct breeds of Catholicism which, for want of better terms, I identified as "Theirs" and "Ours," categories created after observing certain acquaintances.

The former group — intense, mystical, and guilt-ridden — even included a few somber boys who wandered about with their hands clammy and solemnly discussed having "a vocation"; the latter bunch, far more populous, was more concerned with a *va*cation; its Catholicism was snug, intimate and irreverent. Like my buddies, I opted for the latter approach, taking the New Testament at its word: honest mistakes could be pardoned. Interestingly, we're all still Catholics, though none of us is in imminent danger of canonization.

Religion was of course central to the school's curriculum, but it was in general handled lightly and pragmatically by my teachers. Oh, I encountered a couple who seemed to be reincarnations of Jonathan Edwards, but mainly the Christian Brothers offered a thick-wristed piety, oddly comfortable and comforting: everyone was imperfect and everything was forgivable...but don't push it, Buster. By the time I was a senior, religion class was often the site of debates over doctrine and dogma, our doubts rebutted but not quashed. My perception was that narrow canons were finally less important than how you lived.

I remember Brother Raymond, a handsome, husky man with forearms like Popeye's — he always seemed to be surrounded by mothers during parents' nights — telling us that it didn't do any good to roll your eyes to the sky in prayer if you didn't make your life, whether digging ditches or performing surgery, a long, sincere, Christ-like effort to better the world, thus a prayer.

Many of us came from families where mother attended Mass while father attended a neighborhood saloon, so we had identified religion as an interest peculiar to females. But we could in no way view Brother Raymond (or Brother Gerald, or Brother Justin, or...or...or...) as feminine in any sense threatening to our emerging masculinity, so we took his advice seriously, or at least I did. And I still do.

Most of the Brothers certainly seemed to gear their own lives that way, working hard to guide their reluctant, rowdy charges. Many years later I learned that within the order, teaching was viewed in supernatural terms, its performance not distinct from working for the individual Brother's own personal sanctification. I recall especially sitting with muscular, gray-haired Brother Justin, an ex-professional athlete, his jowls dark, his upper lip wet with perspiration as he hunched over a sheet of paper. His eyes were grave as he said, "The test says that maybe sales, or...," he hesitated, "maybe *carpenter?*" — his voice rose because he couldn't believe it. He was trying to interpret a vocational aptitude test I had taken, and the intensity of his concern astonished me. There was no show of masculine casualness, no indeed; this man, who looked as though he could pin Strangler Lewis, was not hiding the fact that he cared about me, about us. In fact, they all did, and that sense of concern remains my strongest memory from that time.

That was all years ago. Today Garces has changed. The Christian Brothers are gone, and so are the Dominican nuns. Its athletic teams were number one in the state last year among schools its size, according to the C.I.F., and ninety-six percent of its graduates matriculated to colleges. But there is much less variety of social caste: far fewer kids like Fuzzy Martinez and Don Maracini, like Quincy Williams and Sal Peña, — fewer fights, fewer farts, and fewer back-of-the-class floor shows. Garces is a prestigious prep school — its rough edge softened by time and affluence. But I find it difficult to imagine that the school could be any better.

I can still hear the muffled echo of gaseous explosions from the back of the room, the roar of Brother Gerald on the attack, the hiss of a dirty joke whispered in the deliciously dangerous environs of a classroom. I can see the student who dressed in black, rolled his eyes heavenward, and pretended he was already a priest, and his afflicted stare when he caught sight of one of those back-of-the-class anatomical displays.

Most of all, though, I remember the certainty and rigor of the Brothers. They were good men and true and I'm grateful to them.

PORTRAIT OF A PAL

There were few other palefaces dancing to Fats Domino's special brand of rhythm and blues that night in 1955, few others jitterbugging across the Rainbow Gardens' floor, few others singing along: "Yes it's me and I'm in looooove again..."

In the dark hall, Raymie Meyer and I and our buddies — Duke, BeeJaw, the Chief, Choosie, and Castro — gathered to one side of the stage as Fats incanted: "Ouuu-ee baby, ouuu-ee! Baby don't you let your dog bite me!" and his music drove toward a peak that caused the mostly black crowd to cease dancing at all. Instead, revelers began assembling in front of the band — a dangerous turn for Meyer and me, two teenage blonds in a sea of ebony. We'd attended enough of these soirees to know it was fight time, and Rainbow Gardens had hosted more Saturday-night bouts than Madison Square Garden.

I lost my beer bravery and decided to become as inconspicuous as possible, sliding somewhere near the middle of my clutch of darker friends — four Chili Chokers and a Blood. Then I heard the Chief gasp, "*Hijole!* Look at your boy!"

In the midst of a raucous piano solo by Fats, a husky towhead had somehow made his way on stage. Grinning, Raymie swayed up to the piano and greeted the star. I immediately began searching for the nearest exit while desperately probing my pockets for rosary beads. All of us poised like sprinters awaiting the gun: at the first hint of general mayhem, Meyer would've been on his own.

Just as two beefy bouncers swung into action, Fats lifted a bejeweled brown hand and they stopped. Raymie continued leaning on the piano, his flaxen hair nearly iridescent in the stage lights, and then he tilted his head back to bay a line or two with Fats. Around us the crowd began to chuckle, then laugh: "Who that fool?"

When the dance finally ended, we skirted a parking lot that had erupted into a battlefield — figures writhing and flashing in car lights, the sharp, wet clicks of fists on flesh like castanets in concert accompanying our retreat. "Man, you *crazy!*" BeeJaw grinned at Raymie once the seven of us had sardined into the Chief's car.

"Yeah, you big dumb German," I accused, "you coulda got us killed!"

He just smiled. "Naw, my boy Fats wouldn't let anything happen to his pals."

"I got your pal danglin'," snapped the Chief.

"That's what we get for lettin' this cat have some beer," BeeJaw said, sounding vaguely awed by what he'd seen.

Unintimidated, Raymie grinned: "*Simón cabrón.*"

"We're gonna give you *Kool-Aid* next time," I said, still timorous.

"Hey, Julio" — my *nom de combat* — "what wrong? You got no *huevos a lo chicano?*"

"*Toma!*" I barked, pumping my arms.

"Hey, you guys better cool it or I'll have to call my boy Fats."

"I got your Fats," the driver responded and this time we all laughed.

I first saw Raymie Meyer when he entered the seventh grade at Garces Junior High School in Bakersfield. As a lofty eighth-grader, I was surveying the new guys when I noticed a clutch of black-haired kids with one blond in its midst. Since we were both out for sports and enjoyed snappy one-liners, we hit it off immediately and have been friends ever since. For reasons neither Meyer nor I understood or cared about then, most of our other pals were Mexican-Americans — rowdy, randy guys devoid of snootiness.

Over the years that followed our social circle remained relatively constant: Dominguez, Alderette, Castro, Williams, Avalos, Peña, Bernal, and Molinaro, among others, speaking fractured Spanish (and fractured English, for that matter), fighting for and against one another, cheering one another's attempts in sports, our lives ebbing and flowing with girlfriends and other diversions but always remaining buddies. We're still *compañeros*, linked by the fact that we entered adulthood together. Ours was and remains the rough male camaraderie of the sweat house.

When Raymie was a junior in high school, he suffered a terrible knee injury in a football game. While he recuperated in bed at home, various of us trooped by with the latest dirty jokes or school gossip, usually in that order, while he dealt pragmatically with the fact that he'd never again be able to play football, no small problem for an athletic kid in Bakersfield then. In many ways it was that period that most clearly revealed the toughness at his core: life was hard but you had to deal with it, and he did. There was no sense that he felt sorry for himself, something reinforced by his large, blue-collar family, which included an aunt, a cousin, and a grandmother as well as his own siblings. Pity was a luxury rich folks could indulge in, and Meyer was a long way from wealthy.

The route that took a bright, working-class kid from East Bakersfield's railroad tracks to the Napa Valley where he is vintner and partner at Silver Oak Cellars was complicated. It began with music as usual (Jerry Lee Lewis: "Drinkin' wine spodee-odee, drinkin' wine!") and a group of us emptying a keg of beer, then trying to walk on the keg, sparring a bit, telling a few spicy tales, recounting imagined athletic prowess, until neighbors called the local constabulary — all in the garage and backyard of the Meyer house on Kentucky Street where we were partying to celebrate a religious event of great moment: Raymie's imminent departure to the Christian Brothers Novitate.

To our collective astonishment, one of our number would enter a religious order. Perhaps as a result of our awe, the party honoring our pal's vocation is remembered as the wildest of the 1950s. Duke and I ended up in a vacant lot being interrogated by gendarmes.

Meyer eventually joined the order, taking the name Brother Justin. He has been Justin ever since, a term of honor and affection that also acknowledges a metamorphosis from his earlier life. Having majored in Spanish at St. Mary's College in Moraga, young Brother Justin first taught high school in Sacramento, then returned to college and earned a graduate degree in enology and viticulture at the University of California's Davis campus. He then served an apprenticeship under the renowned Brother Timothy at Christian Brothers' Winery. Eventually and without rancor — he remains close to his ex-colleagues — he left the religious order, married, and became a successful wine-maker, helping rejuvenate an established but floundering label, Franciscan.

Justin Meyer, vintner, had emerged.

He eventually hatched the idea that there was no reason an American winery couldn't emulate some of its finest European counterparts and produce one superb varietal. "Hey, if the French estates can do it, why can't we? They don't have better grapes or conditions." That realization led to Silver Oak Cabernet Sauvignon, one of the finest wines produced anywhere, if wine critics are to be believed.

How exactly did Justin Meyer, vintner, become interested in the nectar of the grape? I seem to recall a group of us, naive then about the genuine dangers of drink, conducting an informal wine-tasting in Alderette's car, or was it in mine? We were passing around a long dog of white port — it had not been allowed to gasp, let alone breathe — and finding it quite satisfactory. We tried it mixed with lemon juice, a combination celebrated then in a rhythm-and-blues song we all knew by heart.

We tried the "pluck" combined with Dr. Pepper too — mix *that* with Silver Oak Cabernet Sauvignon next time you have friends over. We also developed a taste for another gourmet vino, chanting: "What's the word? *Thunderbird!* What's the price? Fifty twice!"

The memory of those innocent, foolish experiments can even now, thirty-five years later, prompt my liver to scream for help. Drinking was a way to declare your independence in those days and we declared ours loudly. But we didn't all manage to survive: one of our number died of substance abuse and that lesson hasn't been lost on the rest of us. It is perhaps one reason why Justin is a leading figure in the movement to urge that wine be considered and employed as food.

In any case, it came as no particular surprise to me that Justin eventually became what he calls a winegrower (one who grows his own grapes and makes his own wine). A few years ago, when I informed the Chief of Justin's new vocation, he grinned, "I always figured he'd end up a wino."

"That's wine*grower*."

"I got your grower," he snapped.

It's been nearly forty years since I first saw a kid named Raymie stroll onto the campus at Garces. He retains the same generous personality that made him a special friend then, even if his blond hair has departed for Chihuahua and his halfback's figure now resembles a middle-guard's. On one level he remains a tough, earthy kid from the Central Valley, as unimpressed with himself on a personal level as he is impressive professionally. We — Justin, Choosie, Duke, the Chief, all of us — were a generation that had the opportunity to escape the blue collars that encircled our parents' necks. We've done that, but none of us has forgotten who we are or where we came from, least of all Justin.

A few years ago, an aggressive guy at a pool parlor in the bucolic Napa Valley discovered that you can take a boy out of Bakersfield, but.... Full of beer and looking for a fight, the young tough began verbally abusing three comfortable vintners playing eight-ball and minding their own business at the back of the establishment. One of the three warned the miscreant to knock it off. He declined. A few unpleasant moments later, the rowdy found himself deposited in the parking lot and even his phrenologist might not have recognized his gourd. Back in the cafe, the winemakers were once more shooting pool, but one had enriched his legendry and acquired one more name: Call him Spitfire Meyer.

BLOODRITES

As our end tumbled backwards and our linebackers attacked blockers, I sprinted forward to tackle the plunging full-back. He pumped his legs and veered away but I cut off his angle, lowered my shoulder and aimed at his thighs, beginning to clamp my arms even before we collided.

I remember only the impact.

Sometime later, mouth filled with blood, I gazed into the concerned face of a cleric, Brother Justin, who was our assistant coach. He knelt over me as though offering dreamy benediction and I tried to speak but could not. Only fourteen years old, I was playing high school football on a championship lightweight team for Garces High School but this attention was new. I vaguely noted one teammate about my age who looked down at my face, gasped "Jesus," then quickly averted his eyes.

An ice bag was placed on my broken nose. "Can you stand up?" asked the coach, whose own beak featured the tell-tale swoop of a healed fracture.

"I think so." The middle of my face was numb and my vision was still blurred, but I planted first one leg, then the other, under me and swayed there, tasting my own blood before coughing, sheeting my chin with red like a male bird warning rivals.

I hung there for a long moment — willow slim, without a whisker on my battered face — neither boy nor man, then Tom Dugger, our head coach, his eyes shining, grabbed my shoulder pads and said for the entire team to hear, "Good hit!"

Childhood slipped from me like a loose cocoon, and the other players, even the bearded juniors and seniors who had stood back and smirked at my injury, surrounded me: "Yeah, Has', good hit! You *drilled* him, man."

If so, I didn't remember. This was only an intrasquad scrimmage, and I was already a starter at safety. Now, however, tasting my blood and savoring that intonation — "Good hit!" — I had become more, a warrior, and I would with fits and starts remain one, tasting my own blood many times and not always on the field, because I learned that there were worse fates than physical injury: cowardice, for example, was one but fear wasn't; losing wasn't but dishonor definitely was.

Years later, I was inducted into the army, coasted through first basic then advanced infantry training, and when I returned home on my first leave, pals asked me how tough it was. I answered honestly: "Compared to two-a-day practices in August, it wasn't." Ironically, the only major combat I ever saw as a soldier — and I in no way equate it with the horrors of warfare — was on the gridiron. I experience no guilt over not having fought a war because when drafted I reported, and I would have gone anywhere assigned. As it turned out, I was assigned to a football field.

On the wall of my office today hangs a photograph taken in Wurzburg, West Germany, on Thanksgiving Day in 1959. Still slender as a song leader, I stand arm-in-arm with a muscular black man from Mississippi named Richmond Barber, who was my best friend on the Third Infantry Division's team. We appear exhausted. The front of my jersey and pants are stained with blood from my much-broken nose and a dazed grin plays across my face. Rich is more somber, his eyes hooded. We have just completed the final football game of our lives, and we have significantly contributed to a win, 7-0, over a better team.

There is also a certain defiance in that photograph. Racism was rampant among American soldiers in Europe then, and at Mainz a black teammate and I were physically attacked by white GI's at a restaurant for the crime of dining together. Ironically, a Mexican-American soldier, whom we didn't know, came to our rescue. Even then, though, in a game we were as good as our performances: football allowed us more equality than American society at that time encouraged. Rich and I were peers on the field and would forever remain equals off it. The pragmatic egalitarianism of a warrior's urge for victory precluded racism.

There are, of course, many negative things to be said about the excesses of football. It is closely linked to sexuality and it often encourages crudity. It is hazardous and its injuries tend to be cumulative, but that dark, titillating edge is necessary for emerging warriors. As the novelist A.B. Guthrie, Jr. once observed, "Wilderness without some danger is not wilderness at all." As a youthful player, I used football to explore the wilderness of my emerging manhood. Peril came with that territory.

Some people in rural central California during my youth overvalued the sport as others elsewhere do now: even when it is the only show in town, it is not as important as curing cancer or feeding the hungry or disposing of nuclear weapons. Does it build character as some coaches claim? It can, I suppose, but as far as I've been able to observe, athletes by no means automatically become better citizens than nonathletes. And football, especially when and where it is given more importance than it deserves, can certainly cultivate arrogance and insensitivity.

On the other hand, it is fun, featuring rough joshing that constantly tests one's sense of humor. We say we "play" football but in fact we work at it; games are often grim. Still, team camaraderie is rewarding and the locker room, even the practice field, can be realms of frolic: red-hot liniment in a guy's jock strap was one common prank; a teammate of mine had a pair of sweat socks that he swore brought luck, so we substituted a pair of mine without telling him — same luck; freshmen were told that jock cups were nose guards and shown how to wear them.

It doesn't stop at high school. When my dad was playing at UCLA, one of his teammates, Verdi Boyer, made mincemeat of an immense, slow tackle from Washington State; as the game wound down, the battered Cougar finally demanded, "What's your name?"

"Speck Haslam," answered the mischievous Boyer.

When my father entered the tunnel at the end of the Los Angeles Coliseum after the final gun, he encountered a large, livid man hollering, "Where's Haslam? Where's Haslam?"

"A good thing that guy was slow," Pop grinned when he told me the tale.

Hampton Hurt's first pregame meal at New Mexico State became vegetarian when his senior teammates distracted him and his steak disappeared; it remains missing to this day. When Jim Houston was a scholarship freshman at Abilene Christian, he was flattened in practice by an upper-classman, who was in turn remonstrated by the coach: "We got some money invested in this boy, Buster. We'd like him to last at least halfway through the season." Like life itself, football is tough and you learn how to take it or else. A backfield coach once constructively critiqued my play thus: "Pick them legs up, Haslam. You run about as good as old folks screw."

Such incidents mask the fact that this sport really can serve a quasi-religious purpose in a desacrilized community like ours, allowing young males ceremonies that lead them toward manhood. Religious philosopher Mircea Eliada points out that people in archaic societies tried to dwell on what they considered sacred aspects of experience while, in profane societies such as this one, mundane (thus less threatening) perspectives are stressed. What was going on in me, and other kids veering toward sexual maturity, was mysterious, was powerful, was timeless and universal: in a word, it was sacred.

My tribe had long since abandoned circumcision ceremonies and other formal rites of passage; it now treated such an overwhelming change mostly as an inconvenient, perhaps amusing, physical and psychological phenomenon — trivialized and rendered unthreatening in popular culture by the likes of "The Patty Duke Show," "Leave It to Beaver," and "The Ozzie and Harriet Show." In many other cultures, however, this metamorphosis was seen as a sacramental opening, a cusp where everyday life and the deep mysteries of existence merged, and where rituals were not only appropriate but essential.

For an only child like me, raised by a mother who hated and sought to suppress male urges, the masculine rituals of controlled violence offered what I believe was a biologically necessary outlet for at least one of testosterone's urges. Everything from the smell of the training room to running the gauntlet in practice or going nose-to-nose in the pit, everything from the ceremonial taping of ankles and wrists to the prayer before a game conspired to move an apprentice warrior away from one world toward another where deep biological impulses could be channeled, validated, released.

Culture consists of forms that allow us to live meaningfully. Such patterns are vital since they link us with those who preceded us, but they are not unassailable. In fact, we show our respect by challenging and sharpening tribal practices. As a cultural cipher, even in some high schools, football has become profane and empty, too much a steroid freak show attended by uninitiated dreamers who've never tasted their own blood. Spectator sports, to the extent they are merely the domain of fans, can offer only corrupt rituals.

One might argue that fans are also communicants, experiencing catharsis or some such; certainly they experience *something*. Nonetheless, I believe that only initiates are able to appreciate the empowerment to uncertain young men offered by controlled warfare. Too often I've heard folks who never played a down demand — "Why didn't he just hold onto the ball?" — when I knew that the laws of physics made that impossible. A football field isn't a cartoon with plastic bodies and resilient heads: you do what reality allows, no more, and that is all one can ask. In the grandstands it is possible to demand anything; on the field it is possible to do only what your ability and opponents permit.

As the sport moves beyond the level of kids participating, the rank of players thins, the clan of spectators thickens, and that culling process is eye-opening: I was the fastest back on my high school team but one of the slowest on my college squad, although my time had improved. Such sifting can create an athletic elite, unused to constraints socially imposed on others, so it seems to compound football's best and worst aspects until, at the professional level, athleticism and strategy are extraordinary but so can be arrogance and brutality.

I was by no means an elite athlete at any level, but was what the British call a "useful" player. No, having seen future college and professional standouts like Frank Gifford, Bernal Jameson, Jeff Siemen, Joey Hernandez, Jimmy Maples and Curtis Hill cavort on local gridirons, I never harbored the illusion that I was an outstanding performer. But I showed up, pulled on my pads and did what was asked of me. And I suffered some distinct humiliations that were, in their own way, educational.

As a bench-warmer in college, I believed that the coach would one day come to his senses and insert me into a game where I would, of course, save the day. Midway through the season of 1957, I had seen only spot duty at Sacramento State. Then, in the midst of a close game, coach Johnny Baker called my name: "Haslam!" I leaped to my feet, sprinted to him as I fumbled with my helmet, and he said, "Give me your jersey. Leroy tore his and we forgot the extras." Under floodlights in front of 10,000 people, my shirt was stripped and, while my teammates did their best to shield me from view, one more layer of illusion came off with that green and gold jersey. I lived through it.

Lights also shined the night I suffered my most troubling injury. In 1954, playing for the league championship in my final high school game, I was tackled by a defender as I darted through North High's secondary. That play remains kaleidoscopic in memory: cartwheeling into the air after a sharp collision, seeing a flash of stadium lights as I flew, bouncing on the turf but clinging to the ball; I heard the whistle and the crowd's roar as my tumble slowed, then I braced myself and prepared to rise. But a deep, unexpected impact interrupted me, an impact that sucked my mind into my core where pain imploded.

I was carried from the field so shrouded that my mind could not leave that site in my abdomen where the sudden torment of a crushed testicle had drawn it. I literally did not know or care where I was. Our opponents were penalized fifteen yards for the late hit, but that too meant nothing to me as ice was applied and the team physician, not realizing the extent of the injury, advised me to breath deeply.

Eventually pain began to subside and I was able to walk, then jog, on the sideline. In the heat of the moment, I wanted to go back into the game. We were behind 0-7 in the final quarter and driving deep into North High's territory, but it was fourth down and we needed a long five yards for a first.

"Haslam," coach Marv Mosconi said, "we need you to run a quick toss."

He was the coach and he *needed* me to run a toss. I gained only a short five. Neither team scored thereafter, so we lost the game and the title. Ironically, North High, which held me to a mere sixty-five yards in thirteen carries, is my wife's alma mater, located in our home town, Oildale, so most of the boys against whom I played that night were childhood friends.

Twenty years later, I was wrestling with one of my children when his foot accidentally caught my damaged testicle and I again collapsed. Despite two succeeding years of therapy, the ruined organ finally had to be excised. I was by then thoughtful about many things and I could not miss the irony: the sport that had to a great degree given validation to my early manhood had now cost me a chunk of it.

I was low after that surgery, moping and uncertain that my sexual vigor would remain unabated. Middle age had been a time of gradual physical diminution: a ruptured disk had, for example, forced me to stop competitive running when I was forty-one. Now a deeper threat was posed. Where was this old warrior's healing ceremony? It was, of course, within me, for all ceremonies function to concentrate and release the power within.

Two of my closest friends, both ex-football players, began immediate shamanism, via negativa in the manner of males. Jim Gray, a defensive back for San Francisco State and the San Diego Chargers and now a physiologist, said, among many other things, "Man, that must be a record for micro-*micro* surgery, little white dude like you. Hey, you might make the *Guinness Book of World Records*." Another one-time back, now chemist, Pacific Lutheran's Gene Schaumberg, predicted: "Let's see, given your normal level of sexual activity, it'll be a couple of years before you'll be due to find out if what's left of your equipment still works." Well, I didn't wait that long and the equipment was still functional.

The warrior tradition — demanding and enduring — is one of many paths to manhood. Boxing is an even more demanding athletic route and something as simple as performing an adult job competently is another. There are multiple ways

to become a warrior — actual combat being the apotheosis. I
chose the one most accessible during my adolescence: football,
with its rituals (the music, the attire, the incantations), its se-
crets (which I'm not telling), its priests (the coaches), its aco-
lytes (the pep squad), and its oracles (the press). That it also
featured some corrupt priests and empty rituals goes without
saying for it was a human endeavor, no less flawed than the
people involved.   But at its most elemental level, when you
were scared but not cowed, it served as a rough, effective rite
of passage.

It most assuredly forced me beyond my assumed capabili-
ties, teaching me that life wasn't going to be only sweetness
and ease.   Those red badges of courage I suffered were my
versions of a bird's displays, saying I'm male and I'll defend
my masculinity, but they also, perhaps paradoxically, offered a
symbolic parallel with menstruation and its validation of adult
sexuality.   The sport prepared me, too, for inevitable losses —
even of that small orb of amorous tissue.   In truth, though,
I've suffered far more devastating damage to parts of me that
cannot be cut, and I've survived.   Most of all, I've learned that
perfection — going unbeaten in life — is an admirable goal
but an unrealistic expectation. But I've also learned that not to
try — not to go balls out, as we used to say — is itself a be-
trayal.

The worst defeat I suffered as a high school player was
22-0 at the hands of one of California's top teams, San Joaquin
Memorial of Fresno, in 1954.   Ironically, I contributed perhaps
my best prep game that night and would later be named to
the Panthers' all-opponent team.   As the clock wound down, I
was still running hard and an all-state linebacker named Larry
Snyder barreled me into his team's bench as I broke off tackle.
I was untangling myself from various supine Panthers when
Snyder grabbed my shoulder pads and jerked me to my feet.
He outweighed me by at least seventy pounds and was an
immeasurably more gifted athlete but, thinking he wanted
trouble, I thrust my thin chest against his.

"Nice run, guy," he grinned and slapped my helmet.

HOMAGE TO UNCLE WILLIE

Bend, Oregon, 1987:

I helped my uncle from bed into his wheelchair, then through the narrow bathroom door and onto the commode, leaving him there and wandering toward the kitchen for coffee while he did his business. I filled my coffee cup and walked into the dinette, where Jan smiled sadly up at me from the table. "How's Bill this morning?" she asked.

"The same." We touched hands, kissed, then I rubbed her back for a moment. He was my blood kin not hers, but there was a deeper link between them; they had over the past twenty-six years built a great and singular intimacy, he the father-figure she had craved, she the daughter he needed. They were kindred souls. Now his life was drifting, drifting away...he knew it, we knew it...and there was nothing any of us could do except make the best of things there on the lip of the abyss.

"I'll go check Willie," I said — he had always been Willie to his brother and sisters and to me, Bill to everyone else. Although not only Jan but his dedicated step-granddaughter Debbie and a registered nurse named Karen were available, when I was present it became my role to attend to Uncle Willie's bathroom needs. This was unspoken, blood's responsibility to blood: if life itself could not be defended, at least dignity could.

In the bathroom, my uncle had managed to lift his butt slightly and was trying without success to wipe it. He looked up — his head appearing shrunken on the large rack of his shoulders — then reluctantly handed me the tissue. I completed the job, flushed the toilet, and muscled him back onto his wheelchair.

He plopped there and puffed, half of his face blank and drooping like molten flesh, the other half bright and angry enough to melt itself, and said with abject frankness, "I never thought I'd need someone to wipe my ass."

That afternoon, Jan and I bundled him up and the three of us repaired to a locally famous eatery for lunch: blackened catfish, red snapper Vera Cruz, sautéed prawns washed down with a good Sonoma chardonnay. My uncle was a gourmand who years before had taught us, two small-town kids, to love fine food and wine, so that meal was important, a ritual validating our enduring relationship.

With the grace that characterized him, Willie managed repartee with the waitress and something resembling his traditional conversational style: "Glorious salad, isn't it? Utterly glorious."

The following day, we bade him goodbye and returned to California. There were a couple of uncomfortable telephone conversations in the days that followed; then, about a month later, Debbie called and told us that Willie had slipped into a coma. While Jan and I were packing to travel north, she called back.

My uncle was dead.

Oildale, California, 1941:

I remember Pearl Harbor and Willie. He and his brother, my dad, were playing badminton that Sunday morning and I, four years old, was watching. When my mother called them, her voice was strange and she took the time to hurry out to the yard, scoop me up, and carry me into the small house on Arvin Street they then rented. Inside, we all sat around the radio.

I have no recollection of what was said that morning, although I do have a clear memory of tense, hushed tones that frightened me. Everyone in the room had wondered what would happen next: Would the Japanese invade California? Could America rebuild her navy? Would Willie and Pop survive the inevitable war?

As it turned out, my father was deferred — his job in the oil fields was considered vital. His younger brother was not so fortunate. A draftee the previous year, Willie had been out of the army for only six days on that December 7th and would be back in by the end of that month. "It was a short leave," he would say with a wink much later, "but a glorious one." The next four-and-a-half years would take him to the Aleutians, Italy, France and Germany. He would be wounded twice.

Oildale, California, 1945:

In the midst of the welcome-home celebration, Uncle Willie handed me three souvenirs: A Sauer 9-mm pistol (sans firing-pin), a German gas mask in its cylindrical metal container, and a German combat helmet; I have them today. He gave me no war stories, however, never did in fact in the forty-two years that followed.

If asked, he would talk about his service, though not at length, and his tone was usually bemused when he did. The Aleutian service seemed most memorable to him — "Utterly horrible: wind blowing all the time and not a tree in sight" — although what was left of postwar Europe's cultural centers intrigued him too. Not surprising really, since in the manner of people who came to maturity during the Great Depression, Willie was inconsistently educated. He had finished high school and taken a few college courses while working, but had never embarked on a degree program.

He was, nonetheless, a serious reader, aware of and intrigued by western civilization as well as current events and, even before entering the army, he had become an inveterate opera fan — a condition tolerated within our family as an eccentricity on the order of foot fetishism, embarrassing but not evil. It was also good for a few laughs since my uncle was tone deaf. "He can't carry a tune in a bucket," observed my father, no Caruso himself, and it was true; Willie couldn't even hum along to recorded music. Nevertheless, he transferred his love of fine music to Jan and me, but that would happen many years later.

Santa Maria, California, 1951:

At my maternal grandparents' house in my folks' hometown, Uncle Willie talked about his high school athletic career.

"We both went out for track, Speck and me," he revealed, "and we both ran the quarter mile. We'd always sandwich the field: Speck first, me last."

Everyone laughed, then Mom explained, "Your father always looked like he was ready to kill someone when he ran. Bill used to kind of lope in last with a big grin on his face."

Willie nodded, then added, "Of course, Speck was one of the fastest there was in through there." He sounded genuinely proud of his older brother. "An utterly glorious runner. He made it to the state meet when he was only a freshman." I was considerably impressed.

Overshadowed and ignored in the conversation, however, was the fact that Speck's little brother, easy-going Willie, had himself become one of the nation's top swimmers during the early thirties, when he won the Far Western 100-meter breast stroke. My uncle's framed photo was for years the centerpiece in the local swim center's trophy case, but you'd never have learned that from him.

Earlier that very day he had been swimming with a humorous, rawboned woman named Ruby. She was one of a parade of girlfriends he had escorted since returning home from the army. His love life was the subject of seemingly endless family speculation; more than once I heard my mother and aunts discussing it in excited tones. "How was she dressed? No? *Really?* It's certainly time for Bill to settle down."

During that period I was urged to refer to any of Willie's girlfriends as "aunt." It was an ongoing joke that he treated with great good humor. I seldom saw him upset about anything, and me saying "Aunt Ruby" or "Aunt Geri" certainly didn't bother him, nor did my mother's persistent, "When are you going to set the date, Bill?" He'd just smile.

Sunburned and a little tipsy from the beer they'd consumed, Uncle Willie and Aunt Ruby were discussing their adventures at Buena Vista Lake, while my mother and Aunt Marge continued to make none-too-subtle references to matrimony: "Swimming together? That's pretty intimate stuff, Bill. Set the date yet?"

Just then Aunt Ruby, emboldened by the suds she had sipped, said, "Well, Bill rowed us way out to the middle of that darned lake. We were drinking beer and I had to *go*" — my mother's face suddenly tightened and she moved as if to cover my ears, but I grinned — "so I said, `Bill, you've gotta get me back to shore right away.' That *character*, he just kept rowing and laughing, so I showed him."

"You go in the other room," my mother ordered, her voice unambiguous, so I reluctantly slunk toward the kitchen, calling over my shoulder, "What'd you do, Aunt Ruby?"

"I peed in the bailing bucket."

"Ohhh," I heard my mother gasp.

"That really *showed* him," laughed my dad.

"Oh, I didn't *show* him anything. I made him turn his back," grinned Aunt Ruby.

I was by then being thrust into the kitchen by my quivering mother, who hissed, "Don't call that woman `aunt' anymore!"

Oildale, California, 1956:

Christmas Eve and the Tom and Jerries were flowing. My father was always a menace when drinking and that night, true to form, he launched another diatribe against his stepmother and those he believed tolerated her. "I've got too damned much pride to cow-tow to that bitch," he snarled, hinting that his good-natured brother had done just that. Pop never understood why Willie didn't seethe as he did.

"I've got better things to do than to think about her," my uncle explained. "That's all ancient history."

My father would have none of it. "Goddamn it, that woman *abused* us."

"Thirty years ago, my boy," Willie pointed out. "It's all over now."

"The hell it is."

"Well, Speck," commented Aunt Marge, my mother's sister and not one to back down, "no one ever gave your stepmother more trouble than Bill."

"Whadya mean?" Pop snorted.

"I mean the Waldorf!"

Everyone in the room burst into laughter and even my father, after a hesitation, had to smile. "Yeah, maybe," he admitted.

"What's that?" I asked.

"You tell him, Bill," urged Marge.

He grinned. "Well, along about the time dear Mamá" — Uncle Willie often used the word "dear" with satirically devastating effect — "was pushing Pop around pretty good — when was it Speck, 1925, '26? — and she decided that she'd just trump the Santa Maria Inn for some imagined slight and put up a fancy hotel of her own, run 'em out of business, so she had a big sign that said `Future Home of the Santa Maria Waldorf — *Leone Haslam*, Proprietor' put up on one of the lots she owned. Well, a few days later was Halloween, so a couple of pals and I went out to old Dad Hailey's place and borrowed a broken down outhouse he had in through there.

"We loaded it up on the wagon I used to make deliveries from the store and hauled it to dear Mamá's lot, then took down her sign and put up a great big one of our own: `SANTA MARIA WALDORF. *Leone Haslam*, prop. No reservations needed. Quality corn cobs provided.'"

My Mom's mother interrupted him, laughing so hard at the memory that tears were streaming from her eyes. "The one thing that woman couldn't stand was not being taken seriously. I'll tell you, she laid low for awhile after that."

"Then what happened?" I asked my uncle.

"Oh, dear Mamá figured out who had to have done it, so she gave Pop hell and he said I had to haul that privy away right now, so my pals and I loaded it up, that big crowd there to cheer for us, and we paraded through every street in town on our way back to Dad Hailey's. By the time we finished, we'd poked an utterly glorious hole in her balloon."

"You should've seen Bill," added my mother, "sitting there on that wagon with the old outhouse and the sign, grinning and waving to everyone." Her laughter was rich and deep.

"Yes, my boy," smiled Willie, "it was quite a parade."

South San Francisco, California, 1961:

Newly married, Jan and I visited the Bay Area where I had to straighten out a problem with the admissions office at San Francisco State. We were staying with my uncle, by then a widower living alone in a comfortable two-bedroom home. Although I was in my mid-twenties, an army veteran embarking with my wife on a course of studies that would one day lead both of us to degrees, my parents insisted on looking askance at my marriage and on speaking of me as though I was still a foolish youngster: "He'll be sorry."

My uncle took us for lunch at Sabella's on the Wharf and we delighted in pirate's salads — heaps of crab, of shrimp, of scallops on beds of fresh greens; neither of us had ever seen, let alone eaten, anything like them. He walked us through tourist attractions — Chinatown, the Academy of Sciences, Fisherman's Wharf, the DeYoung Museum, the Japanese Tea Garden — and seemed gratified doing so. As Jan would later observe, "Bill's greatest pleasure came from sharing his pleasures." We would continue the jaunts together until Willie moved to Oregon twenty-six years later. Today neither Jan nor I can visit those places without fondly remembering my uncle.

In 1961, however, we were less certain of ourselves, young adults who had chosen to forgo steady employment in the oil fields, the house and car that was sure to follow, and to gamble on the somewhat belated pursuit of education in a large, alien city. Uncle Willie provided our halfway house.

There was no condescension, there were no reservations in his acceptance of us. He allowed us to use his residence as a home base, to live with him until we found a place to rent, and he acted as our advisor when we sought advice; he was our friend, our mentor, our haven. It was clear that he trusted us and had confidence in our abilities to succeed. Although he surely noted unrealistic expectations and foolish performances, he did not admonish. He actually acted upon a belief that we were smart enough to learn from our errors.

Moreover, Willie immediately and without hesitation integrated us into his own jovial and profoundly multi-ethnic circle of friends, which included mixed couples, something we rarely if ever saw in our hometown. My uncle seemed colorblind to a degree unheard of in Oildale, although he and his friends were in the habit of identifying — often inaccurately — everyone ethnically: "When I was in the veterans' *house*pital" — a pronunciation unique to Willie — "there was an Italian boy on one side of me in the ward and a Greek boy on the other. Well, those two got to arguing over this beautiful little Spanish nurse we had in through there...," and so the stories went.

In any case, my uncle's gang congregated at his house most Sundays for lavish spreads of food and drink and conversation. Best of all during those years, he always insisted that Jan and I take all leftovers home, so despite our meager income, we ate well indeed. His friends, especially Ethel and Tom Martinez, also adopted us, giving us everything from slabs of meat to jugs of wine. Never has it been so comfortable to be young and poor and in love.

South San Francisco, California, 1963:

We became parents sooner than we'd planned. As a result, I had to leave school, all but one night course anyway, and work full time while Jan cared for Frederick. There were rumblings in the family that it was time for Gerry to grow up and accept responsibility, time for him to come home, go to work in the oil fields and support his family properly instead of living hand-to-mouth in San Francisco. But my uncle did not agree: "Well, my boy, you two seem set on getting that education, so stay with it. We'll always be able to work something out if you go broke. I have a feeling you two will be good for it." As it turned out we did indeed go broke, he did indeed help us, and we were indeed good for it, all unbeknownst to the rest of the family. With Uncle Willie, our privacy remained private.

Many years later, Ph.D. well in hand, I slipped and revealed to my father that Jan and I had once in an emergency borrowed money from his brother. Pop seemed both hurt and angry: "Why the hell didn't you ask me instead of Willie?" he demanded.

I mealy-mouthed an answer, not admitting that his money dangled strings thicker than octopus tentacles. Willie never imposed provisos.

Every Friday night during the period when I had returned to school to complete my B.A., Uncle Willie had us over for dinner. Those evenings he occupied himself grilling steaks or chops, pouring wine and commiserating at length with my wife about what our golden egg had lately accomplished, about her work — she was then putting me through school — or with favorite topics such as gardening, cooking, and travel. He seemed to have driven every back road in California and to take special delight in discovering out-of-the-way places. Willie also refused to limit his interests to traditional masculine topics: while he was an inveterate sports fan, for instance, he dearly loved flowers and cooking and was gifted with both. I was less flexible, so while he and Jan talked, I'd usually raid his liquor locker, then plop with a beer in the living room to watch television — we had no set of our own, so it was a treat.

One Friday, brew in hand, I sat in front of the TV with Frederick playing in a cardboard box at my feet. He was a happy baby who rarely cried, and I glanced at him with a young father's continuing pride, then at the screen, then back at him. With an uncertain thrust our son suddenly stood in the box, holding onto its sides while his chubby, bowed legs wobbled. "Jan! Willie!" I called, "Come look at this."

Just as his mother and uncle emerged from the kitchen, Frederick let go and stood with perfect pink hands free at his sides, grinning.

A moment later, he plopped onto his bottom and Jan scooped him up and planted a wet kiss on his cheek, so I did the same to her and, for an instant, I felt my uncle watching us. Although he had two stepdaughters, he'd had no children of his own and his marriage had been sadly short; Eleanor, his wife, died only a couple of years after they were wed. There was gravity in his gaze, perhaps wonder, but he too was smiling. That look taught me a volume about what it meant to be family.

Petaluma, California, 1976:

After attending a country parade in nearby Penngrove, we celebrated the Bicentennial in Petaluma, the small town where Jan, our five kids, and I then lived — a traditional barbecue-watermelon-fireworks day. That Bicentennial my wife and I had reason to celebrate the American Dream for we had lived a version of it. We were by then a long way from Kern County's oil fields and packing sheds; my career had blossomed and I was a professor of English at Sonoma State University as well as the author of a couple of successful books. My uncle took great pride in introducing me as "Professor Haslam," and I took even more pride in his obvious satisfaction.

He seemed to be almost the only member of his generation in the family not overly impressed and, consequently, overly resentful about my good fortune. From him I never heard that litany of frustration, "School doesn't teach you *everything*." In fact, our relationship had changed very little. I deferred to him in the many areas of his expertise and he did the same for me. In other realms, most notably politics, we agreed to disagree — Jan and I liberal, Willie conservative — although we often debated our disputed positions without rancor, an unheard of feat in our family. I referred to one of his favorites as Richard "Millstone" Nixon; he called one of mine "President Peanut."

Jan and I shared a passionate commitment to the civil rights movement and disillusionment with America's erstwhile war in Vietnam. We were members of the NAACP and, while Willie was particularly sympathetic with the demands of nonwhites, the specter of lawless demonstrations deeply disturbed him. It seemed to him, and to many good people of his generation, I suspect, that the national fabric was being rent. In his view, demonstrations invalidated even just movements. My wife and I disagreed, feeling that the national fabric was at last becoming a quilt of varied colors and that demonstrations were the only way the disenfranchised could penetrate the nation's consciousness.

Moreover, Jan and I were also Sierra Club members, dedicated, perhaps overly idealistic environmentalists. I was especially proud that Ansel Adams had personally sponsored our membership. We went round and round with Uncle Willie about various matters: "Those loggers have to work. You people've got no right to deny them a living," he'd say.

"They've got no right to destroy unrenewable resources like first-growth forests when there's technology available to harvest other trees."

"Those working people can't put that in their pots."

"But their bosses can. Those're the villains in this thing and they use the loggers as a screen so we can't see the corporate boardrooms and the fat profits."

"Gerald" — I knew matters were deepening when he called me that — "there are hundreds and hundreds of miles of utterly glorious forests in through there. No one wants to harvest all of them, but we can't suddenly change history and economics because your generation living in cities and going to colleges has decided trees shouldn't be logged. The whole economy up north is based on logging and those people have a right to a living. They're more important than trees."

"First-growth redwoods don't have to be logged anymore. There are second-growth forests and tree farms everywhere..." We never agreed on that issue, but when stakes with mylar strips appeared on Mount San Bruno just north of his house, Willie was outraged and we were in total accord.

"Goddamn it, they want to develop every square inch of land in through there. They don't give a damn about the quality of life. Those developers'll say anything to rationalize making more money, their only real goal." He supported the petition that placed development on the ballot, campaigned for the measure, and was delighted when it passed and development was halted.

South San Francisco, California, 1980:

After dinner, the three of us sat around the table sipping the dregs of wine. I winked at Jan as I began to tell a joke. My goal was to prompt my uncle to reciprocate, because he always told dialect stories and all his dialects sounded the same — Other Lingo, I called it.

After I finished my yarn, he launched one: "There was a Jewish boy, a colored boy, and a Portugee boy who got killed and they all arrived at the pearly gates at the same time. St. Peter looked at his book and he said, `I don't know about you boys. I'm going to have to think about whether you get in or not.'

"Well, that Jewish boy said, `Leestena, eefa you leda me eena, I geeva you a meelliona bucksa.'

"St. Peter said, `Wella, thata sounda hokay to me.'"

That triggered laughter, since even St. Pete was speaking Other Lingo.

"That colored boy got in on the action too: `I geeva you *two* meelliona eefa you leda me eena.'

"`Hokay, you geda eena,' St. Peter says. Then he thinks, 'Wella, I might asa wella leda thata Portugee boya eena too.'"

Now St. Peter was even *thinking* in Other Lingo and we were rocking with laughter.

"So Peter asks that colored boy, `Where'sa thata othera boya?' The colored boy looks around and says, `I theenka he looka for a co-signera.'"

By then all three of us were roaring. He could sure tell a joke.

Victoria, British Columbia, 1986:

After another delightful day, I rued my complaint prior to this trip: "We won't have any vacation of our own," I had whined, genuinely aggrieved because our precious and scant private time seemed to be slipping away.

Jan had been adamant. "I told Bill after his stroke that we'd take him to Canada. He wants to go back to Vancouver Island and after all he's done for us, we're taking him." My wife was generally a pliant person, willing to compromise, but for Uncle Willie she was absolutely committed and inflexible.

Just as I was planning a subtle counterattack of spousal sulking, she employed her major weapon: "Remember our last trip to Canada?"

I remembered. In 1965 Jan and I were attending Washington State University and the four of us — two children by then — although much closer to the fulfillment of our dreams, were even more impoverished than before, surviving during the summer on county commodities and what I could earn doing library research for professors. Uncle Willie had driven north with a great CARE package of food, then taken us for a ten-day tour of western Canada at his expense.

My wife didn't tell me how self-indulgent my attitude toward the Canadian trip was; she didn't have to. I, of course, came to my senses. Not only had Jan been correct to make me aware of my selfishness, but she was also correct in her assumption that the journey with Willie itself would be pleasant. It was. He remained an excellent companion and guide, undemanding but willing to explain history and local color as we journeyed to the Island's northern tip, seeing bald eagles and orcas, eating well, and generally relaxing. He told us stories in Other Lingo, placated the sullen teenage son who accompanied us, and made light of his own reliance on a wheelchair: "This damned device doesn't work any better than my lovely legs used to. Of course, it isn't pale, white and skinny." More than anyone I've known, Willie had the capacity to laugh at himself. It was a lesson he taught us through example, and it took.

San Bruno, California, 1987:

My uncle wanted no funeral, but friends and family nonetheless assembled at the veterans' cemetery where he would be interred. His stepdaughter, Sharon, asked me to say something, since I was the closest thing to a wordsmith our family had produced, and I immediately contemplated eloquent homilies. My wife and children were there, and so was my dad, along with various distant relatives and friends of Willie's, so I felt as though I had suddenly been put on the spot. Then I heard my uncle whispering through the chill Pacific wind that whipped us, "Keep it short, Gerald, my boy. Just keep it short."

After everyone gathered around the open grave, I cleared my throat, and simply stated the truth:

"Willie didn't want a ceremony and I'll respect that, but I just want to say that it was my honor to be his nephew and his friend. I'll miss him, we'll all miss him. He was a damned good guy who didn't need fancy words from me. This world is certainly a lesser place for his passing but a better place for his having lived."

Only when I finished did I realize how near I was to breaking down.

Rogue River National Forest, Oregon, 1988:

We are hiking through a cavern of illuminated dogwood and vine maple, sunlit leaves layered like memories as we troop a sandy trail. Occasionally, through clearings to our right, the upper Rogue River appears, slick then tumbling then slick once more. Jan spies two clusters of cadaverous plants beneath ferns on the forest's crowded floor: pale white Indian pipes that are beginning to blacken on their edges. The air is balmy but not hot.

It's a short hike — only a couple of miles — but it's so beautiful that we find ourselves constantly stopping, a little stunned at the lush forest through which we pass. Finally we sense a distant roar. Up a rise, around another bend, then up one more hill and the sound becomes deeper, an ominous shuddering. A few more steps to a rampart and visual intensity at once surpasses sound: the river's course has dramatically deepened and narrowed — sheer lava walls thrusting far below into a river frenzied by that concentration. A cataract explodes where the canyon veers west, and huge, bleached logs are wedged at painful angles into the cratered walls far beneath us but above that cataclysmic current.

Mist rises from below and, across the cleft, the scarred volcanic surface is sheeted with the brilliant green of young conifers poised at disastrous angles, with patches of darker grass and flowers like vivid mistakes on a painter's palette, with kaleidoscopic slashes of lichen and moss. On a shelf just above the frothing water, a line of bright red roots dangles and sways like disembodied arteries.

This place, Takelema Gorge, is one of the most beautiful that a lifetime of hiking and backpacking has allowed me to see. As is often the case in the presence of such natural grandeur, I can find no words. Jan and I stand above the great lava slash, our arms around one anothers' waists. Finally I observe, "Willie would love this place."

After a moment she sighs, "Yes."

We are no longer young. We are no longer poor. But we are still in love. And Uncle Willie remains our point of reference.

DENOUEMENT

Jan is sitting at the dining room table where she works on lessons each morning before departing for school. She had arisen before me, cared for my incontinent father, then started coffee. When I'd later stumbled into the kitchen, she had greeted me with a long hug. Now it is nearly time for her to leave, she has showered and dressed, and she looks as fresh and pretty as she had on our first morning together so many years ago.

Still clad in rumpled pajamas, my thinning hair a wiry disaster, I stop as I often do to gaze at her, to wonder at my good fortune: this beautiful woman is my closest friend, the one indispensable ingredient in my life, and she loves me. How in the world did it happen?

I have no maxims to offer. Jan and I married in the summer of 1961 in Oildale, and I can still feel the heat and turmoil of that signal time, I can hear the admonitions and taste the passions. I did not then clearly distinguish between love and eroticism, and I've no reason to believe she did either.

In retrospect, it seems that we wed out of mutual need, with considerable hope and perhaps a dash of desperation, but with few accoutrements of idealized romance. I liked Jan, lusted for her, but was troubled by her too. Life denied both of us many tender illusions, especially about one another, but in the long run that has proven advantageous: we knew it would take work to build a life together and we have worked. Jan, in particular, has accepted that challenge.

When, the autumn after our marriage, I left my job on an oil-drilling rig to matriculate at San Francisco State College, my young wife took a job as a bank teller to support us. For the next five years, our lives revolved around work and college and kids — we had two by the time I finally began dual careers as a writer and college professor. We had by then carried children to emergency rooms, agonized over strained finances, laughed at our own many small-town faux pas and pratfalls in the big city. We had grown closer and closer.

Neither of us had been expert at marriage, of course, or at much of anything else for that matter, and early on we had some interesting lessons to learn. At first, for example, we thought the man had to be the boss in all matters — that's what we'd heard — so we tried it: not a good plan. Each of us developed spheres of authority within the family. For instance, my wife holds a degree in math and she has for years handled family finances — a fact that astonished and reviled my father, who employed money as power in his marriage.

In truth I'm too lazy to even cash checks much of the time so at home we have an ongoing joke about my chronic impecuniousness. I constantly extend an open palm in my wife's direction and plead, "Do you got a buckaroo?" Her response triggers my next line. It is living theater that tickles our children no end, and we both enjoy it too for we have learned to play together.

It took awhile after we were married for us to really relax enough to laugh jointly, at one another, at ourselves, but we did and it has been another salvation. Most of our worst times have come on those rare occasions when, for whatever reason, we have both lost our sense of humor at once; then even small or imagined transgressions can become problems. Most of the time, however, we deal with difficulties easily.

Back in 1961 each of us had a best friend of the same sex — her maid of honor, my best man — whom we regarded as confidants. They remain our friends but, after a few years with Jan, the notion that "wife" and "best friend" were separate and exclusive categories had departed: she was and is my most intimate confrere. Our relationship began to define and to redefine "love" for me. That process continues.

In my teens, like most of my pals, I was afflicted with what my buddies described as "the flaming hots" for a damsel. It was intense, it was educational, it was painful, but it wasn't love, not as I now understand that condition, anyway. The relationship that has developed between Jan and me, while retaining the flaming hots, has grown into more than I ever imagined: she is my breath. A dimension of intimacy has evolved which I never observed in anyone's marriage and which I never fantasized; it is in no way stifling or limiting.

We have been mutually tempered: a phone call in the night, for example, once informed us that a son had been arrested for a felony; he was later exonerated, but the shared stress of that moment — the look, the touch, the *certainty* that we exchanged — strengthened our mutuality as surely as water sizzling in a blacksmith's bucket toughens a plow blade.

With that same son by our side, we buried our dear old dog, Cloudy, under an oak tree one sunny spring morning. A mongrel, never quite civilized, he was a perfect fit for Jan and me and ours. There was no ceremony, of course, but after laying him in the earth, the three of us stood with our arms around one another, reluctant to close the grave, and I reached down to touch Cloudy's dusty fur one last time, thinking that if there is a Heaven for me it will have to admit this dog, this boy, this woman — theology be damned. Without love, there is no life. At that sad moment as before, my existence was enhanced because Jan shared it.

This deeper realization came to me most fully a few years ago after I spent a summer moping around in the grip of male menopause. I hied myself off on backpacking trips and was generally disagreeable when home. It was a bad time which Jan endured, but I emerged from those dark days with the realization that I had been delusional — perhaps it was my only child's egocentricism re-emerging. My life had been blessed yet I had been determined to *invent* reasons to feel sorry for myself. As I said, I came to my senses and faced hard reality: all my aspirations, all my goals, all my dreams have been realized to at least a degree — all I suppose, except the self-indulgent illusion that I am in any significant way deprived. What a jerk I'd been. Back in 1961 Jan and I were married in a Roman Catholic church and I remain a practicing Catholic, but that is not why we persevere together. With marriages slipping into dissolution all around — Catholic as well as non-Catholic — no institutional affiliation is sacrosanct. No, we're together because we choose to be. Marrying her was the best mistake I ever made.

Earlier this morning I wandered yawning into the kitchen where coffee was dripping and nearly bumped into my wife. "Don't I get a hug?" she asked.

I mock-scowled and demanded, "What's it worth to you?"

Her eyes widened for a second and she smiled slightly, gazing directly into me, stripping thirty years of used tires from my soul; a much younger man surged within me. I hugged her then as I always do, gratefully and with passion.

GROWING UP AT BABE'S

Our last meeting seems, in retrospect, fated. I had not been home for a long while and had not visited the gym for a couple of years, yet that day I drove to Bakersfield determined to catch a workout and banter with one of my few real friends, Babe Cantieny. I had just completed my first year of college teaching and was writing my first book, so I was full of my career; ties to my hometown had not lately loomed large on my mind, but I was determined to correct that.

When I didn't find Babe in the gym, I wandered downtown window shopping until, unexpectedly, I spied him near the California Theater, or him in miniature, for he had shrunken. He was still the well-proportioned, muscular man I had known, but he looked more like a finely conditioned lightweight boxer than a body builder. When I commented on his altered physiognomy, he gave me a crooked smile and said he was dropping a little weight for definition, then we moved to other topics.

We spent most of that afternoon talking, and he uncharacteristically brought up a couple of old misunderstandings, a couple of rough edges in our relationship. Babe wanted, it was clear, to make certain that we had everything in order, but it didn't dawn on me that he might also be saying goodbye. Our conversation, while deep at times, was not morose; we found a good deal to laugh about: the time a greenhorn challenged Charlie Bear Ahrens to a strength contest; the shenanigans we'd observed in the decrepit hotel across the street; the traffic cop who'd finally figured out that I was recycling an old parking ticket on my windshield for nearly a month while I worked out upstairs unconcerned about feeding a meter. It was a good day, one of the best.

A few months later, my mother sent me the clipping from the *Bakersfield Californian* that told me Marion "Babe" Cantieny, local businessman, was dead at 41. Then I understood what had occurred on our last afternoon together. Then, too, I finally admitted how important that short, quiet man had been in my life. I sat for a long time alone on my sun porch, too old to weep, reading and rereading the clipping: remembering, remembering . . .

I had begun lifting weights at Babe's Gym in June of 1954, seven years after Cantieny had opened it near the corner of 20th and Eye Streets. I was a 140-lb. weakling who had not made the football team at Garces High School the previous season. A chum named Charles Tripp convinced me to train there, even though in those days weight lifting was considered hazardous; there were ominous rumors that a few workouts might leave you "muscle bound," unable to tie your own shoes. Still, a friend at Garces, John Renfree, had used weights to go from a pudgy sub to an all-league tackle, and he seemed to tie his shoes with ease.

This was the dawn of the weight-training revolution that has so altered competitive sports. In fact, every athlete I knew in Bakersfield who lifted weights during that period did so at Babe's; he was without question a pioneer in introducing the technique to the area's athletes, especially football players.

Babe, himself, seemed quietly intimidating that first day when Tripp introduced us. All I could see were his bulging biceps as he sat behind his small desk in the cubbyhole he then employed as an office. He was all business as he made out a routine for me and walked me through it. Over that summer he twice altered my schedule of exercises to insure full range of motion and development. I noticed that he was always watching to make certain that all of us did our exercises properly and that no one hurt himself. He was quick to correct flawed techniques, demonstrating them until you grasped the proper method.

Babe had a few close friends among his clientele, chums with whom I'd hear him open up, laugh and romp a bit, but basically he was private without being cold. I realized then that he was far different, far deeper than the brooding adolescents with whom inexperience had at first led me to identify him. His silence was not a threat because he did not need to threaten.

There were rules of conduct at Babe's Gym and they were not breached, not twice anyway. Even in those days when young bucks all thought they had to be fighters, I never saw an argument get out of hand among the youthful studs pumping themselves up. It was clear that nonsense wouldn't be tolerated. Once—this would be in 1957—two large Bakersfield College football players began wrestling among the weights. Babe said only, "Hey!" and they froze. Later, I walked into the dressing room while the two, each appearing twice Babe's size, were gazing at the floor and the proprietor was softly saying something like, "If you can't respect other people's rights, don't come back." They came back but never disrupted workouts again.

The atmosphere at the gym was convivial; as Mike Janzen recently observed, it was like one big family. Babe's Gym remains for me, over thirty years after I first entered it and nearly twenty-five since I've been an active member, my club, the only one I ever belonged to in my hometown, the only one I ever needed. It featured a rugged but not raw male comradery, with joshing and kidding the principal forms of communication. Taking yourself too seriously was not tolerated, although genuine problems were dealt with compassionately.

I especially recall how the older guys shaped up the younger. Once, in my loudmouth youth, I referred to a middle-aged musician's spouse as his "old lady," a cute term that wowed my pals. He turned to me and asked, "Do you mean my *wife?*" I was thirty years younger and twenty pounds heavier than him, but I got the message. "Yes sir," I replied; "Sorry." Doing the correct thing, I learned, was not the same as backing down, and I don't think I've called any woman that again. Mutual respect required, most of all, that it *be* mutual. From such lessons is maturity built. They were taught that way because mutual respect and acceptance were the rule, not the exception—you had to *prove* yourself a jerk in order to be rejected, possibly ejected—which was a reflection of Babe's own personality. If a guy couldn't be comfortable at the gym, he probably couldn't be comfortable.

About 1958, Babe fell on hard times. Big chains of workout salons (we called them "saloons") were opening in town, with high-pressure salesmen pushing "life memberships" which promised profit for the gyms in the guise of bargains for prospective members. The salons featured steam baths and plush carpets and newfangled exercise machines. Babe's customers were dazzled by the dramatically lower rates such joints advertised, and some began drifting away. Moreover, new customers became as rare as saints. Not knowing what else to do, Babe opened a second gym on Baker Street and tried to compete with the chains, even selling life memberships, something that would haunt him for the remainder of his days.

I was inducted into the army that year. When I returned home on leave, Babe had lost his gyms and, to a degree, his self-respect. It was a painful time, because his family life had fallen apart too. But he didn't leave town or hide; he was in fact fighting back, determined to reopen the gym and to try to make good on the memberships that had been forfeited when his business had gone belly-up. "Your reputation is really all you've got," he told me, "and when something like this happens, it seems like everything turns bad, but you can't give up, you've got to work your way back." He did.

I had listened then as later because, without being heavy-handed, Babe had become an advisor to me, and his willingness to acknowledge his own frailties and problems made his counsel all the more valuable. He was the first adult who had ever really confided in me. When I was considering marrying a girl my friends advised against—"It'll never last . . ."—I talked to Babe, who also knew her. He told me about his own failed marriage, and suggested that many of the conventional, romanticized generalizations about marriage were bunk. "Marry someone you can get along with, that's what's most important. You can have the hots for anyone, but be sure you get along. Then put away the past—everyone's got one—and start from scratch. You two will be okay. I think it will work." I married her and, nearly twenty-five years later, remain grateful that I did.

In one limited area, the student became teacher. Babe, like most white men of his generation, harbored misgivings about nonwhites. This is not to say that he was a racist—he certainly was not—but he had little experience with nonwhites and, like many in those unenlightened times, accepted certain stereotypes. In any case, I was, as he once called me, "the resident liberal." We talked often and not very expertly, I'm afraid, about race and ethnicity. Some others in the gym hinted that they'd resent having to work out with nonwhites. When push came to shove and a black East High football player climbed the twenty-eight steps to the gym, Babe signed him up, gave him his routine and, without saying a word, let it be known that he would, like the rest of us, be given the benefit of the doubt.

That occurred, of course, well before the Civil Rights Movement grasped the nation and rattled Kern County, so Babe's act, however insignificant it may seem today, was a long way from business-as-usual then. We talked about that, Babe and I, during our final afternoon together and, while he had by no means joined the NAACP, he acknowledged that I had been correct when I'd urged him to judge each nonwhite as he would each white, individually. I'm glad that I was able to return some small slip of wisdom.

During my initial summer of training at Babe's Gym, once I had realized that Babe was friendly in his quiet way, I'd begun working out during off-hours when there were few others present, and that had led to conversations with him, perfunctory and superficial at first, then deeper and more candid. Eventually I admitted feeling that I had let my father down by not sticking with football the previous year, and he sensed correctly that my too-frequent bravado hid an aching insecurity. He advised me gently and earnestly, then one day asked if I wanted to play baseball. With special friends, when the gym was otherwise empty, he'd pitch a cork—the missile spinning in odd and unpredictable directions—while a batter flailed futilely with a narrow stick. It was a laughing time but, more than that, it was a symbol of acceptance. And if Babe could accept me, I could accept myself.

I played football for Garces the following season, even made a contribution, and I went on to play a bit in college, then in the service, my lean frame bulked up to a massive 165 pounds. I continued lifting at Babe's—except for those years away in the army—until I departed for good in 1961. I still lift three days a week using the routines Babe taught me, at home now with my own kids, none of whom, alas, ever was lucky enough to know Babe. And I still weigh 165; while I'm wearing my hair thinner and my wrinkles deeper, I continue to wear the same size clothing. Best of all, I can still tie my shoes. The habit of fitness came early, and it came from Babe's Gym.

I write this remembrance on Babe's old wall desk, the very one at which he noted in his precise hand my routine that summer afternoon 1954. He gave me the desk when I went away to college and it has seen me through three degrees. Moreover, all of my books, all of my stories, all of my articles—my entire career, really—have been written on it. Like my past and my town and my friends, with all their imperfections, it will do. I don't expect ever to replace it.

WRITING ABOUT HOME

How do you write about home? It's a question that has intrigued me for three decades. Let me begin my answer by defining the key word: *Home* is the place you cannot leave no matter where you go. You carry its imprint in your soul and, no matter how you deny, no matter how you fight to escape, it is there — your truest and most revealing window onto both the particular and the universal. As James Baldwin once observed, "You don't ever leave home. You take it with you." Then he smiled and added, "You *better*."

When critics ask me why I continue to write about Oildale, about Bakersfield, about the Central Valley, I tell them that the place is sufficient, even though my talent or craft may not be. In this site can be found all the great subjects, all the grand dramas, and they are not only themes of my stories and essays, but in a sense they are the settings, too: place and people and passion inseparable as the terrain of the heart. And the heart is our primary locale. As a result, location and purpose often merge, so I employ rural California and its denizens to extol honor or truth or courage just as I use them to attack those narrow, negative attitudes that would bind our souls. Imagination starts somewhere and, since I observed and learned all those things here, I write about them here — an apprentice shaman questing for the sacred.

While attending college in the Bay Area, I learned that the Central Valley did not figure in any significant way in this state's artistic paradigm. Tastemakers there and in the southland ignored Maynard Dixon and Lawrence Tibbett, Mary Austin and William Saroyan, and assigned a gothic bumpkin stereotype to this locale. I knew they were wrong, probably threatened. As William Bevis has pointed out, a region — the very *notion* of regionalism — suggests a margin, something "existing in relation to a center of power." But in the fragmented contemporary world, a region is also subversive, for with it may come rootedness, tradition and values. It resists and mitigates change while the center *subsumes* threatening variations.

The cultural subjectivity manipulated so adroitly by the powerful nonregion, wherever that may be (the Washington, D.C.-to-Boston corridor, perhaps,) is amorphic and determined, capable of absorbing radical chic one day, crying for "law 'n' order" the next. Joan Didion has written "the center was not holding." Of course it wasn't; the center endures by not holding, by conforming and absorbing trends like an amoeba seeking nourishment.

When Saroyan died, a young reporter from the *Los Angeles Times* telephoned me and asked for my reaction. "He was," I said, "a great talent, perhaps the greatest of his time, but a sloppy writer and an irascible guy. If we judge him by his best work, though, he'll be remembered as a major writer."

"But," the reporter protested, "Saroyan's not even in the *Norton Anthology*."

I paused, sucked my breath, then patiently explained: "The *Norton Anthology* no more reflects America's literature than the Chase Manhattan Bank's board reflects this country's population. No, it reflects entrenched power — a safe, unthreatening vision of the country as projected by a controlling elite, and a maverick Armenian from the fringes of society seemed damned sinister. Remember, the center remains the center because it can co-opt what it fears, but Saroyan wouldn't be co-opted; he refused a Pulitzer Prize and made fun of mainline critics. He chose to remain an outsider because his values were real and sufficient, and maybe because he was slightly whacko."

"Oh," said the reporter, apparently unimpressed.

My hometown, Oildale, exists on the margin of Bakersfield, which exists on the margin of the Central Valley, which exists on the margin of California, which exists on the margin of America — if we accept the old paradigm — yet Oildale has proven adequate, and so has the Valley. My model of the golden state, of course, included the rural and small towns I knew well, so I determined with my fiction and nonfiction to write from located experience, perhaps to correct the paradigm that excluded my region from California's artistic map. I was born in this Valley, shed first blood here, fell in love here, conceived my first child here — those are primal realities, not affairs of society or style or opinion. A place is more than observed reality: it is emotion, it is memory, it is the very air you breathe. It dwells as much beneath your bones as it does on the land.

Five years ago, I was approached by representatives of the California Academy of Sciences who wanted me to write the text for a big book — 150 landscape photographs, plus maps and illustrations — on the Central Valley. I didn't hesitate to say yes. In a sense, it seemed to be a project for which my career as a professional writer had uniquely prepared me.

Or had it? Although I had of course published various kinds of nonfiction, I was known primarily as an author of short stories; fiction was my specialty. How did that qualify me to write an extended essay on place? Nearly three decades before, when I was playing college football, I made a discovery. One Monday, watching game films in a darkened room while the coaches droned and the projector clicked, I realized with the clarity of divine revelation that what I was seeing on the screen was not what I had experienced. No, my personal game was invisible to the camera but absolutely true; it had happened on that field but within me. At that moment, I rejected the naive assumption that nonfiction equaled truth while fiction equaled untruth.

Fiction is about actuality but it accepts the challenge of evoking that which cannot be seen, of revealing deeper, sometimes shadowy levels of experience. My training as a fiction writer had indeed trained me to observe and reveal essential if subtle aspects of reality. As a result, I launched into the nonfiction Central Valley project without hesitation, determined to employ the best of both worlds to recapture the region that was my home place. Here's the prologue of the forthcoming book:

> This Valley has rarely been more beautiful than late in the wet winter of 1986. We drive down Interstate 5 toward Oildale in crystal air, past multicolored patches of vegetation flecked with standing

water, a brisk crosswind tugging at our car. Far to the east loom muscular mountains dusted with snow, while closer two rows of aging palms stand as forlorn sentries along a farm road. West of us, treeless hills are emerald now and dotted with muddy cattle.

As we speed south, a fecund aroma rises from the earth, invades and softens, while scythes of sound lift from crow clusters celebrating in the drenched fields. Farther down the freeway, we pass mallards dipping and chuckling in roadside ditches, coots assembling in flooded fields that were once Tulare Lake. Finally, an irrigator, his legs encased in rubber boots that sag like elephant's feet, waves as we pass and I give him thumbs up, then turn and smile at my wife — two Valley kids growing gray but happy and a little startled to be home.

As I wrote that I was trying to capture the *feel* of a homeward journey, not only toward a place but, in a strange way, back into a time that I knew only here — the wonder of discovering and rediscovering yourself and your deepest connections as you slide once more into the place that gave you life. But I didn't want to describe those things because overwriting is a danger, saying too much and tumbling toward hyperbole. Another hazard is fine writing — crafted with more concern for the eloquence of words than for the power of their content. Pretty words alone don't produce memorable passages — hard thinking and deep insights, feelings that resonate with rooted reality, must brace them like studs in a wall.

So I thought about this book and did considerable research. With all that reading, plus the results of over fifty years of personal experience to include, there emerged a considerable challenge of compression. Instead of a detailed history, I decided to include a chapter entitled "Historical Patterns" which presents signal events and suggests symbolic extrapolation.

In April of 1863, for example, the very year Colonel Thomas Baker actually settled at the site of the city now named after his field, a nearby community suffered a death blow. A small village of Tubatulabal, Kern River Shoshoneans, was attacked by troops under command of Captain Moses McLaughlin, and thirty-five Indians were killed. Survivors of the massacre retreated into the mountains or were herded to Fort Tejon, and the village was never again occupied. Meanwhile Bakersfield would thrive; one community born, another destroyed: tragedy and promise a few miles apart — entwined in a dark dance of history.

Moreover, when dividing the Central Valley into subregions, I decided not to follow the classic Sacramento Valley – San Joaquin Valley model. No, I parceled it into its major geomorphic components: Sacramento Valley, Delta, San Joaquin Plain, and Tulare Basin, a more accurate description physically which also more precisely divides this great trough in terms of economy and population. The fate of Tulare Basin is particularly revealing:

> A region of extensive marshes and swamps, sloughs and lakes, it nonetheless captured only six inches of rainfall annually. Millions of waterfowl flew over its dry plains, its alkali sinks, its sand dunes on their way to its wetlands. Hawks might soar above cranes and herons feeding on abundant minnows or lizards.
>
> This anomaly — wetlands amidst desert — developed because five Sierra streams did not drain from the Central Valley but instead puddled in its southern end behind an alluvial fan formed by the Kings River. Mountain snowfall thus created a watery complex in an otherwise arid zone which extended from well above the contemporary towns of Visalia and Hanford south to the wall of the Tehachapi Mountains. From 1860 until 1890 it was known as Tulare Valley, a version of its Spanish name, *El Valle de los Tulares* — the valley of the tules.
>
> William Henry Brewer's survey team in 1863 entered the Basin's northern section where the Kings,

Kaweah, White, and Tule rivers emptied Sierra snow-
melt to form the largest body of freshwater west of
the Mississippi, Tulare Lake; a second, similar wet-
land developed farther south in the Basin near the
present locations of Taft and Bakersfield, where two
lakes — Kern and Buena Vista — collected the flow
of the southern Sierra's longest stream, Kern River.
Between and among those three lakes existed miles
of sloughs and channels, marshes and swamps. None
of this water drained into San Francisco Bay during
normal years.

Extremely wet years, however, might lead to
northern drainage and a single sheet of water —
broken only by high ground that remained as islands
and causeways — could extend from the Tehachapis
to well north of present-day Lemoore, as it did in
1862 and 1890. The symbolic heart of the Basin, Tulare Lake, covered 486,400 acres to depths exceed-
ing forty feet — 120 miles long and fifty miles wide
— in 1862, the wettest year on record. It was surrounded by a band of tules several miles across in
places and its surface was often decorated by large,
floating tule "islands" drifting windblown across it.
By the 1860s when Brewer's party visited, nearly everyone in the state had heard of this remote, fabled
realm, but few had seen it.

Today no one can, because cotton and safflow-
ers and alfalfa are grown where once trout were net-
ted, and the very existence of the West's largest lake
is now only a vague memory. Its slight remains are
impounded in a small evaporation pool. In fact, all
the Basin's lakes are now dry and their beds are lined
by the grids of farms. That fact demonstrates starkly
the dimension of alteration by humans that has occurred in this great trench.

How do you write about home? You can't pander to the
prejudice of editors in Beverly Hills or New York, nor can you

indulge local illusions or pretensions. You do neither the place nor the concept of truth a favor in your writing if you conceal realities about home in order to denigrate it or to protect it from itself. It isn't an artist's responsibility to placate and it isn't in an artist's interest to be intimidated.

Too often folks speak of love and hate as though they are opposites, but as they relate to a locale they are not truly opposed. No, both are manifestations of intense involvement — to love or hate a place is to care deeply about it, whether it be the site of your heart's desire or simply stuck in your craw like a carp bone. You cannot ignore it. The opposite of love and hate is indifference and I cannot be indifferent to the soil that gave me life.

How do you write about home? First, you must achieve perspective — a degree of coolness and curiosity — but that isn't enough. You must also view it as you do a beloved elder — seeing not age but the layering of life, seeing the sum of an existence not merely the results of aging. Then you must write as honestly as your insights and craft allow, admitting and accepting both virtues and flaws. You must grant the place its unique reality on its own terms. As Bevis eloquently states it, "the regional voice, powerful, local, unique, speaks against the faceless center." So, finally and most importantly, you must write from the heart.

In concluding "Oildale," an earlier essay, I tried to embody all those elements:

> ...There is a sidewalk in front of my parents' house, built in 1941 or so says the inscription on the corner. There is also a small parking strip with a tree that has been so brutally trimmed that scar tissue knots it like tumors — a peculiar local style of arboreal coiffure that seems more ritual maiming than practical necessity. Below it, on summer mornings, runoff water from lawn irrigation settles in the gutter, a small pond, and every morning if I arise early I can sit with my dad and watch doves drinking out there — an unchanging reality — dipping their fawn heads, bobbing their white-splashed tails. They

rise with a whir when a truck bounces past on its way to the oilfields. Then the birds return, drink again and occasionally call — a haunting, hollow sound that says "home."

ABOUT THE AUTHOR

Critic David Peck calls Gerald Haslam "the quintessential California writer." Known both as an essayist and author of short fiction, Haslam has edited a series of literary anthologies: *Forgotten Pages of American Literature* (1970), *Western Writing* (1974), *California Heartland* (with James D. Houston, 1978), and *A Literary History of the American West* (with Thomas J. Lyon, et al., 1987). Also in 1987 Devil Mountain Books published his first collection of essays, *Voices of a Place.*

His collection of short stories now numbers five: *Okies* (1973), *The Wages of Sin* (1980), *Hawk Flights: Visions of the West* (1983), *Snapshots: Glimpses of the Other California* (1985), and *The Man Who Cultivated Fire* (1988). He has published one novel, *Masks* (1976).

This spring the University of Nevada Press will release *That Constant Coyote: California Stories* and next winter the University of California Press is scheduled to publish *California Heartland: The Great Central Valley.*